# Voodoo in New Orleans

BY
# ROBERT TALLANT

**PELICAN PUBLISHING COMPANY**
GRETNA 1994

First published by Macmillan
Pelican paperback edition
First printing, October 1983
Second printing, January 1990
Third printing, January 1994

Library of Congress Cataloging in Publication Data

Tallant, Robert, 1909-1957.
  Voodoo in New Orleans.

  Reprint. Originally published: New York: Macmillan,
1946.
  Bibliography: p.
  1. Voodooism—Louisiana—New Orleans. 2. New Orleans
(La.)—Religious life and customs. I. Title.
BL2490.T3 1983        299'.67        83—8261
ISBN 0-88289-336-X

Manufactured in the United States of America
Published by Pelican Publishing Company, Inc.
1101 Monroe Street, Gretna, Louisiana 70053

# Foreword

MUCH nonsense has been written about Voodoo in New Orleans. It seems to me that here is a truthful and definitive picture.

Robert Tallant has done several years' research on the subject and, in addition, has consulted some of the files collected by the Louisiana Writers Project, now in the possession of the Louisiana Library Commission in Baton Rouge, Louisiana.

When I read Mr. Tallant's manuscript I was highly pleased with his accuracy and integrity and I think he has made extremely good use of all his material.

LYLE SAXON

St. Charles Hotel, New Orleans
1944

# Acknowledgments

PARTICULAR acknowledgments are due Miss Essae M. Culver, Executive Secretary of the Louisiana Library Commission, Mrs. Joel Doane Howerton, of Meridian, Mississippi, Miss Caroline M. Burson, Miss Hazel Breaux and Robert McKinney, each of whom, in one way or another, lent assistance.

I want, too, to thank all the people, white and colored, many of whose names I do not even remember, who offered information without which the material for this book could never have been gathered.

And I am very grateful to all those who wrote of my city before me—Alcée Fortier, Charles Gayarré, Lafcadio Hearn, George W. Cable, Henry Castellanos, Grace King, Dr. William A. Read, Charles Dudley Warner, Edward Larocque Tinker, Herbert Asbury and, most of all, Lyle Saxon, to whom my debt is beyond measure.

R. T.

FOR MY MOTHER

# Contents

### PART III · THIS IS THE WAY IT IS

# Part I
# THIS IS
# THE WAY IT WAS

# 1
# Evolution

SOMETIMES a white man in New Orleans takes a walk along South Rampart Street, one of the famous Negro thoroughfares of America. He turns at Canal Street, the city's most important business street, and immediately he finds himself in a new world, with its own particular sights and sounds and smells.

Canal Street is a great wide boulevard, filled with department stores and shops and moving picture theaters. There is the usual crowd of city people, most of them white. South Rampart Street is also lined with places of business and entertainment, but the faces of its people are much darker. Here the white man will seldom see another white face, except for the proprietors and clerks of some of the stores and shops and the other establishments typical of such Negro districts. There are pawnshops, barber shops and beauty parlors, poolrooms and barrooms, night clubs and restaurants, shoeshine stands, small hotels and movies.

Jazz is the sound of South Rampart Street. It comes from every doorway, from every direction—from juke boxes, from the phonographs in the music stores, wherein the customers seem always to be playing recordings made by Negro bands and artists, from radios in shoeshine stands and barber shops, sometimes from an old-time "inner player" piano beyond an upstairs window.

The white man will never forget the smells of South Rampart Street: stale beer and whiskey, oyster barrels too long in the hot sun, hamburgers-with-onions frying on griddles at open windows, a musky mingling of perspiration and cheap perfume, and the curious odor of incense that lingers at some doorways.

The white man walking on South Rampart Street is a foreigner. Unless he has some business errand here he is soon conscious of this fact. He may even begin to wonder if a Negro ever feels as strange when he walks on a white man's street, though he knows Negroes understand white men much better than white men understand Negroes. It seems to the white man that on South Rampart Street the Negro has in his mysterious way built a world for himself, and an amazing and colorful one at that. There is much that duplicates all the streets in which white men conduct and patronize their own business, and much that is very similar to the white men's way of finding recreation and pleasure. Yet there is something else here that is different and of another race.

The white man may feel he is an intruder here, but when he comes to a group of Negroes on the *banquette*—the New Orleans word for what is called a "sidewalk" elewhere in the country—the Negroes step aside to let him pass. Generations of stepping aside for white men bring about automatic reactions. There is no indication of any resentment toward him. There is no hatred in their faces. Neither is there any humility. There is perhaps a little curiosity as to where he is going and what he is doing in the section.

Another thing the white man walking on this street soon observes is that these people have fun. If he is at all intelligent and has had many contacts with Negroes he does not believe them to be "the happiest people on earth." He does not think of them as being "funny." He knows their world is not a minstrel show. He knows they suffer a great deal, that many of them are poor and that they like being poor no more than do persons of his own race. He knows that they are ridden with many superstitions and with many fears. Yet here on their own "main street" they have fun, at least as much fun as do white people on any street with which he is familiar. The stores and windows are filled with things to buy: clothing, usually more extreme in style and color than on Canal Street, but lower priced and certainly more festive; small jewelry shops are in every block; food stores and markets offer good things to eat, and these people love to eat. Restaurants, cafés and bars seem crowded day and night with people having a good time.

But the white man will soon notice other things, and among these will be the street vendors. They are on every corner and often are sprinkled here and there in the middle of the blocks in a careless fashion, as if they are all working together anyway; perhaps they are. They sell toilet articles and beauty aids, products "guaranteed" to straighten kinky hair and make dark skin light, and patented medicines supposed to cure any and all human ailments. They also sell notions and what they call "novelties." If the white man inspects these he will see candles of various sizes and colors, incense and strange-looking roots and herbs, usually reduced to white or brown powders. He will see the empty vials and small bottles these vendors sell, and he will wonder at the sight of the queer old women who stop to buy them. He may even speculate on whether or not these people are Voodoos. He will get no satisfaction asking questions. Here he has reached a barrier. He cannot cross the line beyond which lies the occultism of this South Rampart Street world. Everyone will be polite, but they will tell him nothing—unless he is known to be a white Voodoo.

This is of course based on fear. The white man may be connected with the police—and they know Voodoo is not popular with the authorities. The white man may walk along South Rampart Street as long as he pleases. The people will even step aside to let him pass, but he must ask no questions about its mysteries.

Let the white man linger for a moment before a certain novelty shop only a few blocks above Canal Street. In the window are vials of oils and other liquids, powders of different colors in chipped white saucers, jars of colored sand, packages of incense, and candles of all sorts. On a small dish at the very front is a small gnarled and twisted root with a card before it which states, cautiously, "Johnny the Conqueror, 25¢—sold only as a novelty." The white man won't linger long. Behind him a masculine voice will ask, "Do you want to buy something, Mister?" When the white man turns he will look into the face of a young man who has light brown skin and the smoke-gray eyes quadroons sometimes have. And the white man will mumble some negative words and find himself walking away, without looking back, almost always until he is away from this street and is back in his own white world. It is almost as if some metaphysical force had driven him out of a place in which he did not belong.

That is all the average white man in New Orleans will ever learn about Voodoo. That is all the Voodoos want him to know, unless he is one of them himself. It is so little that he will forget it quickly and will never realize what it is of which he has caught just the merest glimpse.

Time moves swiftly in America. We are young and our ideas of age are somewhat distorted. Fifty years seems very long to us, and a century is almost an eon. We point with great pride to a house or a piece of furniture that is two hundred years old. The coming of the black people and slavery is regarded as being very remote. But there are living persons who were born slaves. All this was yesterday. . . .

Deep in a hidden place just outside New Orleans the black people gathered. Fires blazed along the water's edge, and the beat of huge bones on a skin-covered cask was bass and steady. They stripped themselves of all their clothing and knotted red handkerchiefs together and bound their loins with these. They tied ribbons strung with tiny bells around their ankles. The king wrapped his head in crimson stuff and looped a blue cord about his waist. The queen wore a costume made of fifty red handkerchiefs sewed together, a blue cord like the king's, and a red scarf with a deep fringe.

On an altar was the ornamented box containing Vodu, the Zombi, the holy serpent, and one by one the black people approached the bars set into one side of the box, swearing devotion, pledging secrecy, requesting favors. They took oaths to die or to kill, if necessary, for their god.

This over, the king touched the box with his hand, then seized the hand of the queen with his other hand. Both of them —Mamma and Papa—began shaking and writhing. Papa picked Mamma up and stood her on top of the box containing the snake. Her jerking became more violent. She flung her arms toward the black night sky, and her head rolled on her shoulders as if her neck were broken. A scream ripped from her throat.

Now invocations, curses and sacred words poured from her lips. She was possessed. The god had accepted her as an oracle, and the words she spoke came not from herself but from the snake within the box upon which she stood trembling and jerking.

Papa began the chant: "Eh! Eh! Bomba hen hen!"

The people became infected with the *power*. In a moment they were all possessed. Papa took the hand of the nearest devotee, who in turn took the hand of the person nearest him, and the current of *power* spread like electricity. The chant rose and fell in great crashing waves of sound, as steady and as rhythmic as the tom-toms:

Eh! Eh! Bomba hen hen!
Canga bafie te
Danga moune de te
Canga do ki li!
Canga li!

Papa presented Mamma with the bowl of warm blood from the sacrificed kid. She drank and handed it to each of the people as they whirled past. Her own lips drank the last drops.

The dance grew faster now. They spun and gyrated and leaped high into the air. They fell to their hands and knees, imitating the postures of animals, some chewing at the grass, shaking their posteriors violently. They bit and clawed at each other. Their scanty garments were ripped away. The clouds broke and the moon came out and glowed upon naked black flesh. In pairs they fell upon the hot earth, still panting and gyrating. Some fell unconscious and were dragged away, into the deep darkness of the trees that edged the clearing.

That is the way it was. At least that is the way we are told it was. . . .

# 2
# Li Grand Zombi

VOODOO came to the Americas a little over two hundred years ago. The raids on the African Slave Coast began about 1724, and thousands of these snake worshippers were sold into the West Indies. With them they carried a word, which was the name of their god. The word was "Vodu," and soon, corrupted to Voodoo, Voudou, Vaudau, Voudoux or Vaudaux, it was an all-embracing term which included not only the god and the sect, but all its rites and practices, its priests and priestesses, and the people who obeyed its teachings. The form "Voodoo" is most commonly used now in the United States. Many Negroes, however, have further corrupted it, and refer to it as "Hoodoo."

Yet it is curious that some etymologists give an entirely different origin of the word. They tell us it can be traced to those followers of Peter Valdo—the Waldenses or Vaudois of France—reputed to have used witchcraft and to have practiced human sacrifice, and that it was carried to the French West Indies by early settlers.

The sect spread rapidly. As early as 1782 Governor Gálvez of Louisiana prohibited the importation of Negroes from Martinique because he believed them to be steeped in Voodooism and that they "would make the lives of the citizens unsafe." A decade later Negroes from Santo Domingo were likewise banned.

Life for Negroes in Louisiana under French and Spanish rule was one of concentrated and consistent misery and pain. Their only escape was in death. On the plantations they were worked in chains, guarded by armed overseers; and the whip was applied freely and often. In New Orleans they were worked from dawn until dusk and then were locked in heavily guarded quarters for the night. They were forbidden by law to assemble for any purpose whatsoever and were severely punished, sometimes by death, for the slightest infraction of this law.

Much of this treatment was based upon constant fear of an uprising. These first generations of slaves were savages, brooding and sullen and filled with hatred for their captors. On the other hand, the whites scarcely considered them human. For instance, soon after the founding of New Orleans a slave camp was established in nearby swamps where the Negroes were "broken." Here they were worked and beaten until those who survived were considered tame enough to be sold in the slave markets to plantation masters. This was even carried so far as the selecting of fine male specimens who were used as studs and bred with chosen females so that they might produce children who would bring high prices.

Not only were the slaves punished if caught gathering for dances or for any other reason, but sometimes their owners would also suffer. In 1751 the Marquis de Vaudreuil ruled that any slave owner allowing his Negroes to assemble for any purpose at all with any other Negroes upon his property would be forced to "pay one hundred crowns to the treasury of the Church, and for the next offense of this kind, be sentenced to work for life on the King's galleys." De Bienville's Black Code had previously provided that the Negroes should be branded with the *fleur-de-lis*, whipped, or put to death if they were caught meeting together.

So gathering for Voodoo or any other rites was impossible in those days. Except for a superficial conversion to Catholicism by some masters the Negroes were not allowed to practice any religion at all. It was not generally considered that they had souls.

It was only with the arrival of the American authorities after the Purchase in 1803 that some of these restrictions began to be lifted. Too, by now a second and third generation of Africans had grown up, a generation who spoke the language of their owners and were now more docile, with no memory of savage freedom, and who for the most part accepted without question their status as slaves. With them had also arisen a new generation of owners with a somewhat different attitude toward them. If despotic still, it was less so than during former years and it was in many cases becoming increasingly paternal in its attitude toward the Negroes. Most of the fear of uprisings had dwindled and much of the cruelty had abated. Discipline and punishment were less severe, and the relationship between the two races was growing warmer. Children reared by Negro nurses loved them as they did their own parents and they were served by their Mammies and other household servants with a fierce devotion. Too, slave owners had come to realize that slaves were valuable property and that it was foolish not to take care of their property or to abuse it.

It was at last recognized that the Negroes required recreation, and slaves were allowed to gather on the plantations for dances, weddings and religious celebrations of various sorts, events which the white household often attended, viewed with amusement and provided with some refreshment and encouragement. Sunday became a day of rest for them, as well as the white folk, and religious services were held for their benefit. This, not the Civil War, was the real beginning of the end of slavery.

In 1803 the prohibition against Negroes from the West Indies was lifted and a few years later, when revolution swept the islands and the planters began arriving in New Orleans, West Indian Negroes came in great numbers. This was to be the beginning of organized Voodoo in Louisiana.

For until now Voodoo had scarcely been a living force.

It had appeared again and again, but only to be suppressed with the utmost violence and determination each time it dared to show its face. Plantations were widely separated, and the slaves of various estates did not often meet. Old Negroes passed on a few of the superstitions, remembered a few of the types of *gris-gris* known to their Congo ancestors, but, for the most part, the Zombi was being forgotten. So far as is known there was only an occasional Voodoo gathering in New Orleans until the arrival of these Santo Domingo Negroes. How or why is not very clear, but somehow Voodoo had remained much stronger in the West Indies than in Louisiana. The Santo Domingo blacks had retained their ancient worship almost completely. Their masters, a sophisticated and worldly lot, found New Orleans much to their liking and many of them settled in or near it, instead of in the plantation areas, where their Voodoo slaves would probably have had difficulty in organizing for their ceremonies.

In the city and with the new and more liberal laws they were soon well organized and had converted many New Orleans Negroes, who from then on retained only a veneer of the Christianity in which their owners had reared them.

It is said that the first gathering place of the Voodoos in New Orleans was an abandoned brickyard in Dumaine Street, where they met late at night for their dances and orgies. But the police soon drove them from this place, and it was then that they began to hold forth along Bayou St. John and along the shore of Lake Pontchartrain. Here the king and queen took their places. Here the bonfires blazed and the drums took up their beat. Here were the snake and the sacrifice and the bowl of blood.

There are many versions of these ceremonies. In the original African rite the priestess lifted the snake from the box—it was a python, according to tradition—and allowed it to lick her cheek. From this touch she received vision and *power* and became an oracle. (According to a Dahomeyan legend the first man and woman came into the world blind and it was the serpent who bestowed sight upon the human race.)

In Louisiana the queen sometimes stood upon the box and passed the *power* to the king and the others by merely beginning a chain of handclasping. On other occasions the king lifted the box and shook it, and from the numerous bells which always adorned it came a magic tinkling that induced the hypnotic state desired by the devotees.

Sometimes the god—the Zombi—was also represented by a male dancer. A great caldron would be set to boiling over a fire in the center of the clearing in which the ceremonies were being held and into it would be tossed offerings brought by the members of the sect: chickens, frogs, cats, snails, and always a snake. The queen would begin a chant:

> *L'Appé vini, le Grand Zombi,*
> *L'Appé vini, pou fe gris-gris!*

"He is coming, the Great Zombi, he is coming, to make *gris-gris!*"

A Negro, clad in a scarlet loin cloth, would leap into the center of the clearing. In his hands he carried a small coffin about the size used for a baby. The celebrants would welcome him with cries of *"Li Grand Zombi! Li Grand Zombi!"* as he dropped the coffin at the feet of the queen and began a wild, whirling dance, spinning like a top until he collapsed from sheer exhaustion. Then the others danced, pausing to drink of the contents of the inevitable caldron and quantities of *tafia*, a strong, raw alcoholic beverage. Live pigeons and chickens were sometimes introduced into the rites, to be torn to pieces with the fingers and teeth of the dancers. Sometimes they drew blood from each other, clawing and biting and falling to the ground in embraces of frenzied lust. They were *possessed*. They had the *power*.

What they called the *power* was not all faked, nor was it all caused by alcohol. Make no mistake about that. There took place that transference of emotional electricity from one to the other, until the entire group was a seething mass of magnetic shocks. The same thing occurred among such sects as the Shakers and still takes place, with less bizarre results, among congregations of denominations of the revivalist type.

If a neophyte were present he was subject to certain ceremonies which took place before the actual rites. The king drew a circle on the ground with a piece of charcoal, and the new member was instructed to stand within this circle. Certain fetishes were given him: a wax effigy of a man, a bit of human bone and some horse's hairs. The king would then strike him on the head with a wooden paddle and begin a chant in African dialect, every word of which was repeated in chorus by the others present. At last the neophyte would begin to tremble and jerk. He was getting the *power*. If he stepped outside the charcoal circle the Voodoos would turn their backs on him. It was an evil omen. If he obtained sufficient *power*, the neophyte would pass from the shaking and jerking into a whirling dance, which included wild leaps into the air and yells of elation at his consciousness of acceptance by the Zombi. His dance would continue with increasing speed and violence until he fell to the ground in a dead faint. He was then aroused by the king with a sharp application of the wooden paddle and given the oath of the Voodoos.

# 3
# The Goat without Horns

SACRIFICE and the drinking of blood were integral parts of all the Voodoo ceremonies. Usually it was the blood of a kid that was used, but often it was that of a black cat.

There is little proof of human sacrifice ever having been used in Louisiana. However, the occasional reference to the "goat without horns," an expression common in Haiti and meaning the sacrifice of a young white child, was sometimes heard. For many years Orleanians believed that every small child that vanished had become a Voodoo sacrifice. Add to this the small coffin carried by the Zombi dancer and there gathers a little smoke behind which there may or may not ever have been fire.

There were other scraps of evidence.

The queens were always being accused of kidnapping and murdering children. As late as 1881 there was excitement in New Orleans when a pair of colored parents, both Voodoos, were arrested for suspending their small son over an open fire and beating him to death with a stick. This may have been merely sadism, yet the resemblance to an old Voodoo ceremony of tossing a flayed cock alive into a boiling caldron cannot be ignored.

In October of 1863 there was almost a riot when half of a human torso was discovered in the home of a known Voodooienne. Whispers of the "goat without horns" spread until the newspapers exploded the sacrifice theory with the truth, telling in semihumorous fashion how the anatomical specimen had been purchased by the old Voodoo from a boy employee in a doctor's office.

Those very old Negroes who remember Voodoo rites of other years and remember tales that have come down to them from older relatives nearly always discount the idea. Joe Goodness, very old and black, learned a great deal about Voodoo from his uncle, who was also named Joe Goodness.

"I never saw anything like that and neither did my uncle," he said. "In my day they didn't even drink blood that I know of, but only ate things like gumbo and chicken and drank a lot of liquor. In my uncle's day they did worse things. They used to tear chickens to pieces and eat 'em while they was still alive. They wore all kinds of *gris-gris* tied on their bodies —dolls made out of feathers and hair, skins of snakes and pieces of human bone. I heard people say hoodoos was cannibals and used to eat babies, but I don't believe that unless it was 'way back even before my uncle was alive. I guess it changed a lot, just like it's different now from the way it was when I was a little boy."

Voodoos have always been extremely secretive, especially when white people are concerned. Yet it is said with fair authority that today a third of their members are white, and that, despite all precautions, white people joined the cult almost from its New Orleans beginnings.

The first revelation of this fact took place in 1806. On St. John's Eve of that year a worried white man traced his missing daughter to a Voodoo meeting in Algiers, across the Mississippi River from New Orleans. Here he found her, clad only in a thin nightgown, her hair streaming over her shoulders, waving a wand, while around her danced a hundred half-naked blacks. In the room was a bubbling caldron containing serpents and frogs. The girl confessed she had sought the *power* to regain the affection of a man she loved.

P. Larousse, in his *Dictionnaire Universal du XIX° Siècle*, described a raid by the police on a Voodoo gathering in New Orleans, at which were found fifty nude women, two of them white and prominent socially. The newspapers of the period frequently told of such incidents, and each St. John's Eve the reporters seem to have discovered such mixed groups.

St. John's Eve is the most important date on the Voodoo calendar. On this night, which has had religious significance since those ancient times when the sun worshippers rolled their blazing wheel down a hill to celebrate the sun's descent, the Voodoos always gathered for a great conclave. Joe Goodness told of the St. John's Eves he remembered.

"They sure did carry on," he said. "There was always a crowd of 'em out by the lake. They had a big altar on the ground and the snake and lots of food. The queen would get up there wit' nothin' on but a few handkerchiefs and a blue cord around her waist and do her number, and it was sure somethin'. Now they tell me you see all that stuff in shows, but then it was a religion. They'd have chickens and cake and they drank rum and anisette. The queen would put a picture of St. John on the ground and that really started the meetin'. Everybody would kneel down and knock on the ground three times. That was for Faith, Hope and Charity. Then they'd get up and start doin' the Creole dance.

"In the Creole dance each man had two women, one on each side of him, and they'd all have rings on their knees that would make noise when they'd move around. The man would turn one woman first, then the other one. That was the Creole dance. After a while, when it was gettin' late, the queen would give the signal and they'd strip off their hand-kerchiefs and run out into the Lake. Man, then it was everybody for hisself. They sure did cut up! Sometimes people was so drunk and excited they got drowned. The water was just about up to their shoulders, but they'd fall down and get stepped on."

Asked about the attendance of white people at these affairs, Joe Goodness admitted that they had participated on some occasions.

"There was a Voodoo queen named Helen Thomas who always had a couple of white women at her dances," he said. "They'd carry on and shake worse than the colored ones. I don't know if they believed in it or just came for a good time, but I've seen 'em dancin' the Creole dance wit' coal-black men. That wasn't no more than sixty years ago.

"I can remember the Congo Square dances on Sunday afternoons, too," he said. "People thought they was Voodoo dances and it's true that a lot of the people who danced there was Voodoos, but they really wasn't the real thing. The regular dances wasn't ever held in public."

The dances in Congo Square were the direct result of the attempts of the city authorities to combat Voodooism after the coming of the Santo Domingo Negroes.

New Orleans had been an American city perhaps a decade when the dangerous aspects of Voodoo congregations began to impress the public officials. The idea of a racial uprising became again important. It was known that the Voodoos were stirring up hatred against their white masters and that some of their meetings were held for the purpose of working black magic against the whites, if not to plot actual revolution. In 1817 the Municipal Council issued an ordinance forbidding slaves to gather for dancing or any other purpose except on Sundays and only in places designated by the Mayor. Congo Square was established as the recognized place for such dances and, under police supervision, it was here that the Negroes met each Sunday afternoon for more than twenty years. The Voodoo gatherings along the lake continued as always, but in Congo Square they held their "legal" dances.

Congo Square was in the very heart of the city, situated on North Rampart Street where had stood the ramparts of the old city. Today, renamed Beauregard Square, it holds the Municipal Auditorium, but once it was occupied by Fort St. Ferdinand, one of the settlement's principal defenses. However, the fort was gone when it was turned over to the slaves. At that time it comprised two city squares and was a green plain containing only a few large sycamore trees. Surrounded by a picket fence which held four gates, in the very center was a cannon that was fired at nine o'clock each night as a curfew for all slaves. Any slave caught on the streets after that hour was arrested unless accompanied by his master or bearing a written permit. All this, of course, was a further precaution against rebellion.

But the slaves made the most of the time allowed them, and each Sunday they crowded the small park. The actual dances were held not in the square now known as Beauregard Square, but in the one beyond it, now occupied by houses. Here, while the white people gaped through the picket fence, they performed the Calinda and the Bamboula and other dances of a relatively mild character, omitting the more grotesque and sensual features of the lakefront gatherings, and they wore not their red loincloths, ankle bells and knee rings, but all the castoff finery they had been able to coax from their masters and mistresses. Sometimes they did attach metal rattlers to their legs, and this and the Congo drums always in use were the only music needed. The current Voodoo queen was always present, of course, the most elaborately dressed woman, the haughtiest and the most carefree. For the Voodoo queen was never a slave, but always a free woman of color who need fear neither the curfew nor any of the laws applied to slaves.

They did sing the Voodoo songs, but most of these the white public could not understand—even when they were mocking the whites—and it considered them as harmless as the popular half-Congo, half-Creole: "Dansez Calinda! Badoum! Badoum!"

The songs and chants used in old Voodoo rites are almost forgotten now. George W. Cable wrote of a chant which was shouted at the climax of the ceremonies: "Aie Aie! Voodoo Maignan!" Cable also recorded the following chant, given him by Lafcadio Hearn, and which he offered in phonetic French, there being no other spelling:

> *He-ron mandé*
> *He-ron mandé,*
> *Tigui li papa,*
> *He-ron mandé,*
> *Ti-gui li papa,*
> *He-ron mandé,*
> *He-ron mandé,*
> *Do se dan do-go.*

Gottschalk, famed New Orleans composer, compiled much Voodoo music and it is said to have pleased Chopin. In its queer strains may perhaps be found the rudiments of jazz, for New Orleans is the home of Jazz as it is of Voodoo and they may easily have a common origin. Most Voodoo chants and songs were hummed or whined *sotto voce* with an effect that was barbaric and exotic and added to the hypnotic design of all the ceremonies, despite absurd and childish words.

A song given to a reporter of the New Orleans *Times-Picayune* was printed in that newspaper on March 16, 1924. Probably a very old one, it reflects the dominance of the queens in New Orleans Voodoo and boasts of their tremendous *power*. Originally sung in the *patois* known as Creole, it is given here in English:

> They think they frighten me,
> Those people must be crazy.
> They don't see their misfortune
> Or else they must be drunk.

I—the Voodoo Queen,
With my lovely headkerchief
Am not afraid of tomcat shrieks,
I drink serpent venom!


I walk on pins,
I walk on needles,
I walk on gilded splinters,
I want to see what they can do!


They think they have pride
With their big malice,
But when they see a coffin
They're as frightened as prairie birds.


I'm going to put *gris-gris*
All over their front steps
And make them shake
Until they stutter!


    Voodooism seems to have been a matriarchy almost from its first days in Louisiana. The king was always a minor figure. Papa didn't count. Mamma was the entire show. The only men of importance were the witch doctors. The king was probably changed from year to year and was actually the current lover of the queen. Women seem, too, to have made up at least eighty per cent of the cultists, and it was always the female of the white race who entered the sect. When white men were present it was usually because they sought handsome yellow girls rather than for reason of any belief in the Zombi. Nearly all the songs were about the queens. The following, in Creole, told of the greatest of all Voodoo rulers, Marie Laveau, of whom much will be told later, and boasted of how she had gone to school with the crocodiles and of how much *power* she possessed:

*Eh, Yé, Yé Mamzelle,*
*Ya, yé, yé, li konin tou, gris-gris*
*Li, ti, kowri, avec vieux kikordi;*
*Oh, ouai, yé Mamzelle Marie*
*Le konin bien li Grand Zombi!*
*Kan sôléid te kashe,*
*Li té sorti Bayou,*
*Pou, apprened le Voudou,*
*Oh, tingouar, yé hén hén,*
*Oh, tingouar, yé éh éh,*
*Li appé vini, li Grand Zombi,*
*Li appé vini, pol fé mouri!*

These were the songs the white people heard when they came to Congo Square on Sunday afternoons; gay, childish, absurdly boastful words sung to savage rhythms. The white people watched and often laughed indulgently at the pleasure their slaves were having. All they saw and heard looked innocent enough. They heard rumors of the other affairs out by the lake, but they only half believed them. This was all nothing but Negro foolishness.

Yet sometimes they were given cause to wonder. An early morning stroller in Congo Square would come upon a rooster tied to a tree. The tortured creature would be alive, but it would be plucked of every feather and sticking in its breast would be nine silver pins. On other occasions someone would find a rooster dressed in a coat, trousers and a hat. Occasionally a plate of *congris*—black-eyed peas and rice cooked with sugar—would rest on the dewy grass under one of the sycamores, surrounded by a ring of silver coins.

Even now, in modern Beauregard Square, such things are found once in a while. In 1943 a white boy of fifteen was passing the Auditorium and, happening to look down, saw something beneath the evergreens in front of the building. When he investigated he found a plate containing roast chicken, rice, green peas and turnip greens. At one side was a saucer of tomato salad, at the other a plate of French bread and butter. Around the dishes silver coins had been arranged in a neat circle. Having no fear of Voodoo, he pocketed the coins and went on his way. At the corner he stopped in the grocery store of Mrs. Sam Gramer to buy some candy. Mrs. Gramer has never forgotten that.

"Oh, my God!" she will tell you, always making the sign of the Cross. "I still think about that child. I begged him to take that money back and leave it where he found it, but he just laughed at me. I know something terrible is going to happen to him because those hoodoo people left it there. I feel it in my bones. I never did believe in all that, but, say what you like, it's something to leave alone. That poor little boy. He was as pretty as a picture on a wall, too. It's such a shame!"

# 4
# Skin a Black Cat with Your Teeth

CONGO SQUARE was closed to the Negroes some twenty years after being assigned to them. Once again fear of an uprising had become epidemic. However, in the 1840's it was re-established as their place of recreation and continued as such until the outbreak of the Civil War.

By 1850 the New Orleans newspapers were defending the Voodoos, probably because the sect provided them with colorful copy more than for any other reason. In July of that year the *Weekly Delta* editorialized as being "inclined to question police rights to interrupt their rites. . . ." On this occasion the police had arrested a large group of women—white, black and of mixed color—while they were gathered for a Voodoo dance and proceedings which those making the arrests described as indecent and orgiastic in character. These women, for one of the first times in Voodoo history, refused to admit the charges made against them. On the contrary, they summoned eminent counsel, who argued in excellent form that such Voodoo practices were purely religious and that the law had no justification for its attitude toward them. In order to justify the arrests, the court, apparently bewildered at this unexpected and unheard-of situation, seems to have been compelled to fall back upon an ordinance forbidding the assembling of white women and slaves.

From then on the Voodoos made life complicated for the police. In August of the same year the *Times* described the arrest of about fifty nude women, including several white ones, who had been found dancing together in the Voodoo tradition, and described the queen, when she appeared at the trial, as a "dusky Venus," whose "influence over the ladies of her court was as powerful as a Voodoo spell." This entire trial seems to have been a farce. The white ladies claimed they had been unclad only because of the excessive heat and had been present only because they had one and all collapsed simultaneously on the doorsteps of the Voodooienne. They were fined and dismissed.

Then, just a few days later, on August 13, there appeared an account of a girl who claimed to have been "hoodooed" and was, she vowed, suffering under a spell. She gave birth to a child and said it was all caused by Voodoo and that the birth was the result of an immaculate conception.

In 1855 a Voodooienne, one Elizabeth Sutherland, was mobbed by her neighbors, who believed she had placed a spell upon them. The police rescued her and bore her to the comparative safety of the Third District Station. However, a crowd soon gathered outside the station and insisted upon meting out to her the fate due a witch. Desperate, and faced with the problem of either becoming accessories to Voodoo and finding themselves the butt of newspaper gibes or having a Salem scene in New Orleans, the police at last spirited Elizabeth out a back door, then solemnly told the waiting mob that she turned herself into a black cat and leaped through the bars of her cell!

Voodoo queens now became increasingly brazen. When Betsy Toledano was brought to trial she expressed astonishment at the charges lodged against her. A "stout and intelligent free woman of color," according to one newspaper description, she declared that she held her position as a Voodoo queen through rights of inheritance. Acting as if she thought the police were, if not entirely lacking in intelligence, certainly devoid of appreciation, she proudly displayed some of

her *gris-gris* in court and boasted of complete faith in her
*power*. According to a newspaper, Betsy seemed quite sincere
and "contended she had a perfect right to hold meetings of
the Voudou Society . . . that the Society was a religious
institution which had been transmitted to her, through her
grandmother and mother, from the ancient Congo Queens."
The court, even with the evidence Betsy herself exhibited
frankly, the horsehairs and pebbles and pieces of animal bone,
seems to have had a difficult time in establishing a charge of
holding an illegal congregation of slaves.

Another Voodooienne of the same period found herself
in trouble with the police when Julia Henderson, a prostitute, died of black cholera and her friends brought charges
against Hoodoo Mag as having caused her death by supernatural means. The *Daily Crescent* referred to this witch as
"a black hellcat named Margaret, a slave belonging to Mr.
Marpolise, and known to Negroes throughout the city as
Hoodoo Mag, the queen or high priestess of the mystic order
of the Voudous. . . . The priestess claims to have the exclu-
sive business of compounding and retailing bags containing
charms and bottles containing direct curses. . . . Not only
Negroes, but white women, are known to belong to this
infernal institution." Nothing more was heard of Hoodoo
Mag. The charges were of course ridiculous and her master
probably delivered her from her difficulties.

During the war years of the 1860's the newspapers had
other things to write about and Orleanians other things to
think about. But the next decade brought renewed interest
in the Voodoos.

A reporter for the *Times* was present at a St. John's Eve
celebration in 1872, and on June 26 he published an account
of it, which described how shocked he was at

. . . the sudden entrance of a hoydenish flaxen-haired white girl,
who whirled around the room in the arms of a negro blacker than

the ace of spades. . . . There could be no mistake about it. Set adrift on the rapids of depravity in real earnest, she had reached the center of the vortex. The pallid wanton face actually beamed with exuberant levity, and La Dame aux Camelias, in her wildest hours, could not have displayed an abandon more complete. Even the negresses gazed at her with a look of wonder. While the maddening whirl continued our reporter watched the wretched creature, as one after another the ebony suitors sought her hand; he saw her shrink out into the darkness, and more wanton than ever rush back to the revel, and mute with amazement he also turned away.

He concluded the account with the remarkable observation that "these Voodoo orgies can scarcely be deemed improving to the refined or cultivated."

Despite the attempted secrecy, more and more people seem now to have been locating and viewing the Voodoo ceremonies. Voodoo had become a topic of conversation in the lush drawing rooms of the Creoles and St. John's Eve seems to have been an occasion for groups to go searching for the gatherings. We are told that on some occasions the roads along the bayou and those going toward the lake were choked with carriages. Creoles and other Orleanians sought the services of Voodooiennes, sometimes for a lark, sometimes with great seriousness, and it was everyone's desire to witness a Voodoo rite.

Howard LeBreton, a very old colored man, recalled the crowds that attended a Voodoo dance in 1875.

"This one was out by Lake Pontchartrain," he said, "and thousands of people come out to see it. I can remember it good. The Voodoos danced on barges on the water just away from the shore and they carried all kinds of torches and lighted candles. The queen was dressed in a long purple dress with a blue cord 'round her waist, and all her co-workers wore purple dresses, too. And they didn't wear nothin' underneath. Them was what they called good-time dresses. The

men wore white pants wit' purple shirts and they carried
white candles.

"You never seen such dancin' in your life. They all danced
first slow, then faster. They would go 'way down to the
ground and come up shakin'.

"On the barges they had statues of saints and altars and
lots of stuff to eat. They had wine and beer and everybody
got drunk. It was just like a picnic."

Despite all this, Howard contended that white people did
not see all the Voodoo meetings. "There was some nobody
but the real Voodoos ever seen," he said. "People didn't know
that, but it's the truth."

The reporter who described a St. John's Eve affair some
years later, in 1896, gave a blunt and somewhat cynical description of the festivities. He does not seem to have been
either shocked or impressed. "The rites," he wrote in the
*Times-Democrat*, "consisted in building a large fire, in a dance
on the part of a central personage, the destruction of a black
cat and its devouring raw. The scene concluded with an orgy,
in which the savage actors ended by tearing off their garments." Voodoo had now been a part of New Orleans life
for nearly a century and perhaps this gentleman had been
seeing such rites for years.

Grandma Beavois, a Voodooienne of the present time, an
old black woman with white hair and but one very belliger-
ent eye, insists the black-cat rite is still performed on certain
occasions.

"Papa Felix is the only man left in New Orleans what can
do it," she said, "and he's a hard man to meet. Papa Felix
don't never mess wit' strangers. I seen him skin a black cat
lots of times. He gits a crowd in his kitchen for a meetin' and
somebody brings him a black cat wit' its feet tied together.
He puts a tub of boilin' water on the table and lights candles

all aroun' it. Then they says the prayers and sings the Voodoo songs and Papa Felix keeps turnin' the cat 'round and 'round wit' its head hangin' down and it screamin' and goin' on like a black devil. Then, all of a sudden, he plops the cat down head first in the boilin' water. When he pulls it out it's dead as a doornail. Then he holds it up and there is a lot more prayin' and shoutin'. He takes his teeth and bites clean through the cat's throat and skins it complete wit' his teeth. After that they eat the flesh and divide the bones. Black-cat bones has lots of *power* and makes good *gris-gris*."

The old woman plunged a hand into the pocket of her apron and exhibited a tiny bag made of dirty red cloth. She untied a bit of string and emptied the contents into her hand. There was a piece of black stone that looked like coal, a snail's shell and a fragment of glistening white bone. "That from a black cat's tail," she said. "Papa Felix give it to me. It's my protection."

As the Voodoo ceremonials evolved from the primitive African rites Christian and particularly Roman Catholic features were incorporated into them, creating the queer mixture that exists today. C. D. Warner, touring the South near the close of the nineteenth century, viewed a meeting which had many of the Catholic features grafted upon its Voodoo base. It began with the reciting of the Apostles' Creed, which was followed by prayers to the Virgin Mary. A statue of the Virgin stood upon the altar. Aside from this, though, there was little about it that was Christian. Warner published an excellent description of what he saw in his *Studies in the South and West*, part of it as follows:

The colored woman at the side of the altar began a chant in a low, melodious voice. It was the weird Danse Calinda. A tall Negress, with a bright, good-natured face, entered the circle with the air of a chief performer, knelt, rapped on the floor, laid an offering of candles before the altar, with a small bottle of brandy, seated herself beside the singer, and took up in a strong, sweet voice the bizarre rhythm of the song. Nearly all those who came in laid some offering before the altar. The chant grew, the single line was enunciated in stronger pulsations, and other voices joined in the wild refrain,

> Danse Calinda, boudoum, boudoum!
> Danse Calinda, boudoum, boudoum!

Bodies swayed, the hands kept time in soft pat-patting, and the feet in muffled accentuation. The Voudou (the witch doctor) arose, removed his slippers, seized a bottle of brandy, dashed some of the liquid on the floor on each side of the brown bowl as a libation, threw back his head and took a long pull at the bottle, and then began out in the open space a slow measured dance, a rhythmical shuffle, with more movement of the hips than of the feet, backward and forward, round and round, but accelerating his movement as the time of the song quickened and the excitement rose in the room. The singing became wilder and more impassioned, a strange minor strain, full of savage pathos and longing, that made it almost impossible for the spectator not to join in the swing of its influence, while the dancer wrought himself up into the wild passion of a Cairene dervish. Without a moment ceasing his rhythmical steps and his extravagant gesticulation, he poured liquid into the basin, and dashing brandy, ignited the fluid with a match. The liquid flamed up before the altar. He seized then a bunch of candles, plunged them into the bowl, held them up all flaming with the burning brandy, and, keeping his step to the maddening "Calinda," distributed them lighted to the devotees. In the same way he snatched up dishes of apples, grapes, bananas, oranges, deluged them with burning brandy, and tossed them about the room to the eager and excited crowd. His hands were aflame, his clothes seemed to be on fire; he held the burning dishes close to his breast, apparently inhaling the flame, closing his eyes and swaying his head backward and forward in an ecstasy, the hips advancing and receding, the feet still shuffling to the barbaric measure.

Every moment his own excitement and that of the audience increased. The floor was covered with the debris of the sacrifice—broken candy, crushed sugarplums, scattered grapes—all more or less in flames. The wild dancer was dancing on fire! In the height of his frenzy he grasped a large plate filled with lump sugar. That was set on fire. He held the burning mass to his breast, he swung it round, and finally, with his hand extended under the bottom of the plate (the plate only adhering to his hand by the rapidity of his circular motion), he spun around like a dancing dervish, his eyes shut, the perspiration pouring in streams from his face, in a frenzy. The flaming sugar scattered about the floor, and the devotees scrambled for it. In intervals of the dance, though the singing went on, the various offerings which had been conjured were passed around—bits of sugar and fruit and orris powder. That which fell to my share I gave to the young girl next to me, whose eyes were blazing with excitement, though she had remained perfectly tranquil, and joined neither by voice nor hands nor feet in the excitement. She put the conjured sugar and fruit in her pocket, and seemed grateful to me for relinquishing them to her.

Before this point had been reached the chant had been changed for the wild canga, more rapid in movement than the *chanson africaine*:

> *Eh! Eh! Bomba, hen! hen!*
> *Canga bafio, té,*
> *Canga moune de le,*
> *Canga do ki la,*
> *Canga li.*

At intervals during the performance, when the charm had begun to work, the believers came forward into the open space, and knelt for treatment. The singing, the dance, the wild incantation, went on uninterruptedly; but amid all his antics the dancer had an eye to business. The first group that knelt were four stalwart men, three of them white laborers. All of them, I presume, had some disease which they had faith the incantation would drive away. Each held a lighted candle in each hand. The doctor successively extinguished each candle by putting it in his mouth, and performed a number of antics of a saltatory sort. During his dancing and whirling he frequently filled his mouth with liquid, and discharged it in a spray, exactly as a Chinese laundryman sprinkles his clothes, into the faces and on the head of any man or woman within reach. Those so treated considered themselves specially favored. Having extinguished the candles of the suppliants, he scooped the liquid from the bowl, flaming or not as it might seem, and with his hands vigorously scrubbed their faces and heads, as if he were shampooing them. While the victim was still sputtering and choking he seized him by the right hand, lifted him up, spun him round a half a dozen times, and then sent him whirling.

This was substantially the treatment that all received who knelt in the circle, though sometimes it was more violent. Some of them were slapped smartly upon the back and the breast, and much knocked about. . . .

While the wild chanting, the rhythmic movement of hands and feet, the barbarous dance, and the fiery incantations were at their height, it was difficult to believe that we were in a civilized city of an enlightened republic . . . it was so wild and bizarre that one might easily imagine he was in Africa or in hell.

As I said, nearly all the participants were colored people; but in the height of the frenzy one white woman knelt and was sprayed and whirled with the others. She was a respectable married woman from the other side of Canal Street. I waited with some anxiety to see what my modest little neighbor would do. She had told me that she would look on and take no part. I hoped that the senseless antics, the mummery, the rough treatment, would disgust her. Towards the close of the séance, when the spells were all woven and the flames had subsided, the tall good-natured negress motioned to me that it was my turn to advance into the circle and kneel. I excused myself. But the young girl was unable to resist longer. She went forward and knelt, with a smile on her face and a candle in her hand. The conjurer was either touched by her youth and race, or he had spent his force. He gently lifted her by one hand, and gave her one turn around, and she came back to her seat. . . . In the breaking up I had no opportunity to speak further to the interesting young white neophyte; but as I saw her resuming her hat and cloak in the adjoining room there was a strange excitement in her face, and in her eyes a light of triumph and faith. We came out by the back way, and through an alley made our escape into the sunny street and the air of the nineteenth century.

Mr. Warner locates this ceremony as having taken place in the upper portion of a house near the Congo Square. He does not identify the witch doctor.

# 5
# Doctor John

THERE are few names so important to the history of American Voodoo as that of Doctor John. A huge black man, a free man of color, himself an owner of slaves, he claimed to be a Senegalese prince and the masses of grotesque scars that marked his fierce face were believed to support this claim.

John told an exciting, almost fantastic story of his life. He said his father had been a great king and had marked his son's face in the traditional custom of their royal family. But the Spaniards had come and he, John, had been among those stolen and sold into slavery. At last he had become the property of a gentleman who was traveling to Cuba, and on that island he had grown to manhood, had become an excellent cook and had finally coaxed his master into granting him freedom. Then he had worked on sailing vessels, visiting all parts of the world, even making a trip to Senegal, where he found his father had died and the life there not to his liking. John then returned to the sea, eventually quitting the ship in New Orleans, where he went to work as a cotton roller on the docks. It was during this period that he began to discover his *power*. His employer, noticing that the other Negroes feared him, made him a sort of overseer.

As his fame spread and he learned more of the tricks he realized that many people were willing to pay for his services. He saved his money and bought a property on Bayou Road and built himself a house. He began purchasing slaves, all of them female, and some of these he married, performing his own ceremonies. Later he boasted of having fifteen wives and over fifty children. He soon became someone at whom people stared in the streets, for he owned a carriage and pair as fine as any possessed by any white gentleman, and a blooded saddle horse, on which he rode through the streets, attired in a garish and elaborate Spanish costume. Later he forsook all this for austere black and a frilly white shirt front and affected a beard.

His home contained a conglomeration of snakes, lizards, embalmed scorpions and animal and human skulls, the last stolen from graveyards. The last woman he married was white and she presided over the establishment, with the fourteen black ones kept quietly in the background.

Like most of the witch doctors he left the meetings and the dances to the queens. If he attended them it was mostly as an onlooker. He specialized in healing and the selling of *gris-gris* and the telling of fortunes. To his cottage came thousands. He placed and lifted curses for a fee. He combined pseudomedical practices, astrology and divination with pebbles. Fine white ladies, heavily veiled, sought his advice regarding their love affairs and bought a tiny bottle from him for a fabulous price. Many a young beau and aging cavalier paid a large sum for a shell wrapped in a twist of human hair or a packet of talcum powder, to be used in winning the favor of some girl, perhaps white and rich and acceptable socially, perhaps quadroon and beautiful and desirable. Parents sought his aid for the protection of wayward sons or daughters. Sick people sought health, and old men and women sought youth. There were, too, those who paid him regular sums through sheer terror of some secret knowledge that he held.

What few of these people knew was that Doctor John employed scores of Negroes who worked in the homes of the most prominent families as servants. To Doctor John they sold certain information—or gave it to him because of some hold he had on them. It is safe to say that this hideous man knew more of the private affairs of the "best" families of New Orleans during the 1840's than any other living person. When dignified men or women of prominence sat in the dark and odorous little house, surrounded by all the horrible paraphernalia of the witch doctor's profession, and heard their innermost affairs and thoughts described to them by this sinister Negro with the tattooed face, they could not but be impressed. And they paid dearly for his knowledge. Blackmail? He never made threats, but they thought it best to pay. They never guessed his sources, but believed he could read their minds and their souls.

It was the white clients who enriched him. "One would stand aghast," wrote Henry C. Castellanos in his book, *New Orleans As It Was*, "were he told the names of the high society dames, who were wont to drive to this sooty black Cagliostro's abode, to consult him upon domestic affairs. As he was well informed of many family secrets, through the connivance of family servants attached to the cause of Voudouism, his powers of vaticination cease to be a subject of wonder."

He had many names: Doctor John, Bayou John, Jean Montaigne and others. More than anything in the world he hated mulattoes. "They're neither white nor black," he would always say. "They're mules." And the many shades of colored folk in New Orleans paid dearly for this antagonism toward them.

At least one living person remembers seeing Doctor John. Nathan Barnes, who in 1944 believed himself to be about 85 years old, and admitted that he had been practicing Voodoo all his life and still makes a good living from it, told of seeing the Senegalese at a St. John's Eve ceremony.

"He hardly never went to them," Nathan said, "but I seen him there that night. He was a man about the age I am now

and I believes he was kind of broke and low by then. Marie
Laveau was queen then and people say she learned a lot of
tricks from old John Bayou. The time I seen him he was still
tall and straight and had a white beard. He was leadin' the
singin' and beatin' on a barrel covered wit' oxhide wit' two
horse's legs. He was old, but he was strong and you could
hear his voice two miles away. I never did forget that, and
I recollect thinkin' that when I growed up I wanted to be
jest like old John Bayou.

"A little while after that, a man took me to his house. He
was livin' wit' some of his children then that was from his
white wife and was mulattoes. He sure did hate 'em. He told
me, 'Son, thank God you is black. I got children that ain't
nothin' but mules—jest plain mules.' I was hopin' to learn
some tricks from him, but I was too scared to ask and he
didn't tell me nothin'. When I left he gave me a big tooth
that had come from a mad dog, and he tell me to keep that
as long as I lived 'cause it would give me *power*. You know
I done kept that all my life. Lots of times people tried to *fix*
me, but it never did work. You know, when they *fix* you
that mean they done put bad *gris-gris* on you.

"I recollect one other thing about old John Bayou. One
time I lived across the street from a woman that used to wake
up in the middle of the night and find her house bein' show-
ered wit' stones and bricks. That happen every night for a
week. She got the police and they watch, but nobody couldn't
never find out where them rocks was comin' from. They jest
come out the air like they was throwed by somebody what
was invisible. 'Course we all knowed it was spirit work, but
nobody knowed how to stop it. The poor woman cried all
night long and all her doors and windows was busted and
she made up her mind to move. The police was runnin' 'round
like they was crazy. Well, one day somebody told her to go
see John Bayou, and she done it. He promise her she ain't

never goin' to have that happen again, and it never did. Jest like that it all stopped. He was powerful and he could do anything."

Doctor John was brought into court on several occasions in connection with such showers of rocks and stones, apparently propelled by supernatural forces, in the neighborhood of his residence, but he always offered a foolproof alibi and proved that he had been far from the scene of the poltergeist disturbances. Police always were summoned and were always completely baffled at the sight of rocks flying through the air before their eyes, apparently from out of nothingness. No one was ever caught throwing them. However, Doctor John could stop them, and did—for a fee. One case on record tells how the slaves of a Mr. Samuel Wilson paid the sorcerer $62 for such a service. Mr. Wilson went to court and the sum was disgorged from Doctor John. A few days later, according to the *Daily Delta* of October 21, 1867, heavy stones again rained upon Mr. Wilson's front gallery.

The man with the tattooed face is said to have accumulated a neat fortune from his Voodoo practices, though he knew nothing of business methods and could not read or write. It has been said with fair authority that at one time he had $150,000 buried on the grounds of his property. He had a reputation for being very generous with his poorer neighbors, and, whether it was for purposes of advertising or out of genuine charity, he distributed bowls of gumbo and jambalaya to these people, many of whom did not always have enough to eat unless they received such help.

But in the end his lack of and scorn toward all schooling was his ruination. As he grew old his money became a burden and he found it increasingly difficult to manage his affairs. He would not trust a bank with his cash and could not be convinced that once he had turned over his money to such an institution he would ever see it again. He made a few in-

vestments in such small businesses as grocery stores in his
neighborhood—and the stores always failed. Some of his wives
and grown children began to disappear, and with them always
went some of his cash. People cheated him out of money by
promising to invest it for him, and he never saw them
again.

At last he decided that he must learn to read and write
and thus become better able to handle his affairs. He employed
a young Negro to teach him, and spent long hours learning
to sign his name. Then he was one day persuaded to sign at
the bottom of a blank sheet of paper. With that signature
went his Bayou Road home, all his property, everything he
possessed.

He could never understand what had happened to him. He
tried to regain his fortune in lottery, but he was unlucky.
Then he made several attempts to regain his prestige as a
Voodoo, but younger people had taken over his clientele. At
last, at about eighty years of age, he had to accept shelter
with some of the children his white wife had borne him—
mulattoes such as he had always despised. It was as if the
great Doctor John had himself been *fixed*. Death came shortly
after that.

"In the death of John Montanet, at the age of nearly a
hundred years, New Orleans lost, at the end of August, the
most extraordinary African character that ever obtained
celebrity within her limits," wrote Lafcadio Hearn in *Harper's
Weekly* of November 7, 1885. Hearn cited the Voodoo's
aliases as having been "Jean Montanet, or John Fecelle, or
Jean Bayou, or Voudou John, or Bayou John, or Doctor
John." Hearn was, however, mistaken about his age. He was
actually about eighty-two years of age. For some reason aged
Negroes are always "nearly a hundred" in writings of the
period, probably because they themselves are fond of exag-
gerating their ages.

Doctor John left indelible marks on Voodooism. He had broken a great many of the traditions and was one of the first to mix Catholicism and snake worship. In his home there had been a statue of the Virgin Mary, though he probably considered it of less importance than his dried toads which hung from nails in the walls of his front room. He was the first to devote most of his powers to the reading of the future and to healing. He was the first to establish his agents throughout the city. He may have been the first to practice his sort of blackmail.

It is said that he confessed to intimates that he believed in none of the black magic he practiced. He had been known to laugh when he told of selling a gullible white woman a small jar of starch and water for five dollars.

Yet this may not have been entirely true. "He was in many respects a humbug," wrote Hearn, who had talked with him on many occasions, "but he may have believed sincerely in the efficacy of certain superstitious rites of his own. He stated that he had a Master whom he was bound to obey; that he could read the will of his Master in the twinkling of the stars; and often of clear nights the neighbors used to watch him standing alone at some street corner staring at the welkin; pulling his woolly beard, and talking in an unknown language to some imaginary being."

In any case, whatever he was, or whatever his powers, New Orleans missed the sight of his tall figure, always dressed in solid black, except for the immaculate ruffled shirt front and the white beard. There was not to be another Doctor John.

# 6
# Some Were Evil

DOCTOR YAH YAH operated in New Orleans during the same period as Doctor John, and though he was less well known he seems to have had a clientele of considerable proportions. He violated the tradition that all Voodoo leaders were free, for he was a slave, whose real name was George Washington. From the little that is known of him it is evident that he imitated Doctor John and added little to the practices. He was present at many of the meetings held near Lake Pontchartrain. His talents included fortune-telling and "healing." His career came to a sudden end in 1861 when he was jailed for selling poison to an Italian fruit dealer, who, fortunately for him, had taken the potion to a chemist before accepting it as a cure for his rheumatism. Doctor Yah Yah's master paid a fine, obtained his release and shipped him off to end his days toiling in the undignified role of a field hand on a plantation.

Doctor Jack, also operating during that period, is the only Voodoo on record who ever scared himself to death. This magician, who was especially noted for his love charms and was well attended by seekers after that most popular of diversions, offered for sale beef hearts, perfumed and decorated with toads' feet, spider claws and satin ribbons like valentines, which were supposed to be particularly efficacious in matters involving the affections. Whether because he had faith in them himself or because he liked to sleep among his own creations is not known, but Doctor Jack always slept with one of these hanging over his bed. One night it fell on his face and he woke with such a shock that he completely lost his senses and died three days later.

Doctor Beauregard arrived in New Orleans from Kentucky in 1869 and was one of the few "foreign" Voodoos to succeed in the city. He was probably the most amazing of all the witch doctors in appearance, having long hair that reached nearly to his knees, but which he usually wore done up into a number of strange knots. In these he carried all his *gris-gris*, bottles and packages of oils and powders, dried reptiles, tiny bones and a hoot owl's head. Once, after scaring some ladies on the street, he was arrested and he tried to frighten the police by throwing the hoot owl's head at them and screaming curses upon them and their offspring to the fourth generation. Evidently their *gris-gris* was stronger than his. He went to jail. When he was released he disappeared. Evidently he had returned with his talents to Kentucky or had sought new fields.

Don Pedro is usually named as the successor to Doctor John, but not much is known of him, except that he was constantly embroiled with the police because his home was so often the scene of sexual orgies in which white as well as colored women took part. On at least one occasion a police raid led to much scandal and subsequent tragedy. Castellanos wrote of this event in 1895:

The organization of the Voudou, as an organization, has been suppressed in great measure by the efforts of our municipal authorities. . . . Many of the old residents remember the "Racket Green," along the St. Bernard Canal, where thousands were in the habit of congregating to witness the battles of the "Bayous" with the "LaVilles," in the games of Raquettes. The field was an immense one, extending from Claiborne as far back as Broad. In the center stood an old pottery, apparently untenanted. While the game was progressing, the Captain, aided by a strong corps, advanced unobserved upon the dilapidated tenement and arrested the whole concern—Voudous and paraphernalia—while engaged in one of the wildest orgies that most prurient imagination can conceive. The women, having cast off their everyday apparel, had put on white camisoles—called today "Mother Hubbards"—and were all found clad in this uniform attire. Blacks and whites were circling around promiscuously, writhing in muscular contraction, panting, raving and frothing at the mouth. But the most degrading and infamous feature of this scene was the presence of a very large number of ladies (?), moving in the highest walks of society, rich and hitherto supposed respectable, that were caught in the dragnet. Two of them, through consideration for the feelings of their relatives and connections, so unexpectedly brought to shame, were permitted to escape, while the husband of a third, unable to survive the disgrace of his wife, deliberately took his life on the following day. These facts . . . were the subject of town gossip for many a year.

The Raquette Green, now long vanished, was for some years a favorite meeting place for the Voodoos of New Orleans.

Joseph Melon was a witch doctor who was, despite all his magic, unlucky in love. Not all the *gris-gris* he possessed could make the woman he wanted reciprocate his desire. Lily Lamrest told this story. The girl Joseph Melon courted was her aunt.

"He was a big Voodoo around town," she said. "It was before I was born, way back when Marie Laveau was living, but my ma told me about it. He used to always pass her house and she would meddle him; you know what I mean—she would laugh at him and make fun. One thing I gotta give my ma is that she wasn't never afraid of no hoodoo.

"He was a funny kind of fellow, my ma said. He always carried a book and a walking cane, and he would holler at my ma in Creole, 'Hey, Cecile! I'm going out and jump in the lake,' and my ma would scream and whoop at him. One day he pass and he saw my aunt after she had come to live with my ma, and she was young and kind of good-looking, and he fell for her right away. He would bring her a big red apple every day like, but my ma wouldn't let her eat any because she was afraid they was *fixed*. She say she didn't want no hoodoos in our family. Anyhow, my aunt already had a fellow.

"Well, after a while my aunt would run inside every time she seen Joseph Melon coming, and he knew that she wasn't ever gonna love him. Then he got mad and he *fixed* her in a different kind of way. She and her fellow broke up and she never did get another one. She died an old maid, and it was Joseph Melon who done that to her. She wouldn't love him, so he wouldn't let nobody else love her.

"He had lots of mean tricks. When somebody done him something or he wanted to cross them, he would cook a big pot of *congris* and at night he would go to where they lived and throw some of it in front of their door and the rest on the four corners of the block they lived in. Then he would go to Congo Square, to a big tree, and throw three nickels in a hollow in that tree with the person's name written on a piece of paper nine times. Then he would dance around the tree all night long. People came from all over to watch Joseph Melon doing a *sangre*. He was terrible. But my ma said he was kind of nice-looking, too."

But, for all their influence, the witch doctors were secondary to the queens. For some reason the women always ruled. The witch doctor often assisted at the larger ceremonies, but the queens ruled the meetings.

Despite this, there are few authentic records of the early queens. There are probably two reasons for this. The first is that a single name, that of Marie Laveau, reigned over the

Voodoo world nearly seventy-five years. The other is that
prior to that the sect had been subject to many schisms and
changed rapidly from year to year. There is also the fact, of
course, that in the early years there was so much secrecy and
perhaps the Voodoos themselves did not always know the
true identity of their queen.

Sanité Dédé is the first queen of whom there is anything
known. One of the Negresses brought from Santo Domingo,
she is said to have purchased her freedom through secret
Voodoo practices, probably by earning sufficient money in
that way. However, for years after that she sold sweetmeats
in front of the Cabildo in order to support herself, so she
could not have been so successful financially. It was she who
presided at the brickyard in Dumaine Street and she was probably the first to lead a band of cultists into the habit of holding their gatherings on the shore of Lake Pontchartrain. Her
*power* was at its zenith in 1825, and that year a fifteen-year-
old boy viewed one of her ceremonies. Years later, when he
was grown, J. W. Buel described the scene in his *Metropolitan
Life Unveiled, or the Mysteries and Miseries of America's
Great Cities,* recalling that:

An entrance door was opened at the call of Dédé, and I witnessed a scene which, old as I am, no passage of time can ever
dim. . . . Each man and woman had a white handkerchief tied
around the forehead, though the heads of the latter were covered
by the traditional Madras handkerchief, with its five, nay, its
seven points, upturned to heaven. There were males and females,
old and young, Negroes and Negresses—handsome mulatresses
and quadroons. With them half a dozen white men and two white
women. . . .
Near where I stood was on oblong table about eight feet in
length and four in width. On its right end stood a black cat, and
on its left a white one. I thought them alive, and having a certain
fondness for cats, stretched out my hand to stroke the nearest . . .

they were fine specimens of negro taxidermy. . . . In the center of the table there was a cypress sapling, some four feet in height, planted in the center of a firkin or keg. Immediately behind the cypress, and towering above it, was a black doll with a dress variegated by cabalistic signs and emblems, and a necklace of the vertebrae of snakes around her neck, from which depended an alligator's fang encased in silver.

At the side of this table I recognized an old Negro by the name of Zozo, well known in New Orleans as a vendor of palmetto and sassafras roots; in fact, he had a whole pharmacopoeia of simples and herbs, some salutary, but others said to be fatal. He seemed to be the corypheus of these unhallowed rites, for the signal of the beginning of the work came from him. He was astride of a cylinder made of thin cypress staves hooped with brass and headed by a sheepskin. With two sticks he droned away a monotonous ra-ta-ta, ra-ta-ta-ta, while on his left sat a Negro on a low stool, who with two sheep shank bones, and a negress with the leg bones of a buzzard or turkey, beat an accompaniment on the sides of the cylinder. It was a queer second to this satanic discord. Some two feet from these arch-musicians squatted a young Negro vigorously twirling a long calabash. It was made of one of our Louisiana gourds a foot and a half long, and filled with pebbles.

At a given signal the four initiates formed a crescent before Dédé, who was evidently the high priestess or Voudou queen. She made cabalistic signs over them and sprinkled them vigorously with some liquid from a calabash in her hand, muttering under her breath. She raised her hand and Zozo dismounted from his cylinder, and from some hidden receptacle in or behind the great black doll, drew an immense snake, which he brandished wildly aloft. . . . He talked and whispered to it. At every word the reptile, with undulating body and lambent tongue, seemed to acknowledge the dominion asserted over it. In the meantime, with arms crossed and reverent eyes, the initiates had now formed a crescent around Zozo. He now compelled the snake to stand upright for about ten inches of its body. . . . Zozo passed the snake over the heads and around the necks of the initiates, repeating at each pass the words which constitute the name of this African sect, "Voudou Magnian."

Hardly was this last ceremony over when a long, deep howl of exultation broke from every part of the shed. Zozo went back

to his tam-tam, his accompaniers right and left, and the gourd
musician with his rattle. A banjo player, too, sprang up, and pan-
demonium was unloosed. . . . Zozo, leaving his tam-tam, went up
to the altar . . . and again drew forth the snake. He forced it to
wriggle and writhe over and around the company, uttering the
words which were repeated by sixty voices, "Voudou! Voudou
Magnian!" He then twirled the snake around his head and dex-
terously cast it into the blazing pile. Such a yell as arose no words
can describe. The rude instruments took up their discords, mixed
with yells. The chorus of Dante's hell had entered into the mad
shouts of Africa. . . . Up sprang a magnificent specimen of
human flesh—Ajona, a lithe, tall, black woman, with a body
waving and undulating like Zozo's snake—a perfect Semiramis
from the jungles of Africa. Confining herself to a spot not more
than two feet in space, she began to sway on one and the other
side. Gradually the undulating motion was imparted to her body
from the ankles to the hips. Then she tore the white handkerchief
from her forehead. This was a signal, for the whole assembly
sprang forward and entered the dance. . . . Under the passion
of the hour, the women tore off their garments, and entirely nude,
went on dancing, but wriggling like snakes. . . .

The orgies became frightful. Suddenly the candles flared up
and went out, leaving nothing but a faint glow from the dying
pyres. I had grown sick from heat, from an indescribable horror
that took possession of me. With one bound I was out of the shed,
and with all speed traversed the yard. I found the gate open, and
I was in the street and near home sooner than I can tell. If ever
I have realized a sense of the real visible presence of his majesty,
the devil, it was that night among his Voudou worshippers.

That is the only picture we have of the cult under the rule
of Dédé. It is almost the only description we have of any
of the pre-Laveau queens.

Little is known, for instance, even of the rather important
Marie Saloppé, who immediately preceded Marie Laveau. It
was from her that the great Laveau received her training, and
it is believed that for a time the two ruled jointly over the
St. John's Eve ceremonies.

There are those who say Marie Saloppé became Zozo LaBrique, a well known New Orleans street character, an apparently half-demented creature, who peddled buckets of brick dust. She was *fixed*, they say, by Marie Laveau because the latter wanted to rule the Voodoos alone. It has long been a custom among some New Orleans housewives to scrub their front steps with brick dust, a tradition having a definite connection with Voodoo—the washing away of an evil omen placed on the house by an enemy. It is true that now many people will tell you that they do this only for reasons of cleanliness, yet that was its original meaning, and many stoops in the poorer section of the city have a well scrubbed, whitish appearance, showing that brick dust has been used. Zozo LaBrique sold her dust for a nickel a bucket, and when she died a small fortune in those coins is said to have been found in her disreputable quarters.

But, whatever happened to her, it can be understood that Marie Saloppé had to go. Marie Laveau was coming!

"Marie Laveau?" said an ancient Negress, still cooking for a family in the French Quarter. "Sure I heard of her. I don't know if she was good or bad; folks says both ways. But I know this: she was a *powerful* woman."

# Part II
# MARIE LAVEAU

# 7
# Marie
# the Magnificent

WILLIE THOMAS, an aging Negro who thought he was close to ninety, claimed to remember Marie Laveau well. "That was around 1885," he said. "I went to some of her meetings and sometimes I sang with the Voodoos. Marie Laveau was the most beautiful woman I ever seen in my life. She was banana-color and she always wore gold hoops in her ears that made a pretty sound when she walked. She had nothing at her meetings but white men and yellow girls, and they danced naked all night long."

The trouble with that story is that there is absolute proof that Marie Laveau—at least the first Marie Laveau—died on June 24, 1881, at the approximate age of eighty-five. Willie Thomas could not have remembered her.

The legends abound in every section of New Orleans. Aging memories offer as many versions of the identity and characteristics of Marie Laveau as there are vaults and tombs in St. Louis Cemetery No. 1, where it is both vowed and denied that she is buried.

Marie Laveau, they say, was ruling the Voodoos in 1830. In 1895 she is reported as presiding at a meeting near Bayou St. John. At least one old woman vowed solemnly that Marie Laveau lived until 1918, until after World War I. The newspapers, reporting her death in 1881, stated with complete seriousness that she had reigned over the Voodoos for eighty years. Lafayette is said to have kissed her forehead when he visited the city. Nearly a century later gossip had her the mistress of Lafcadio Hearn!

22 *Voodoo in New Orleans*

The truth of course is that there were at least two Marie Laveaus. There may have been more. There is evidence that a dynasty was established in an attempt to pass the rule of the cult from mother to daughter. It seems also to have been a deliberate attempt to found a legend of immortality.

The first reliable record of the first Marie is that of her marriage, in the files of the St. Louis Cathedral. The contract reads as follows:

> Paris, Jacques (quart. lib. illeg.) a native of Jeremias, St. Domingo. Son of Jacques Paris and Blou Samitte, married Laveau, Marie, a native of New Orleans, illegitimate daughter of Charles Laveau and Darcantel, Marguerite, Aug. 4, 1819.

The ceremony was performed by Père Antoine, a cleric beloved in New Orleans history, who for fifty years was one of the best-known figures in a city then almost entirely Latin and Roman Catholic, and who at his death, ten years after Marie's marriage to Jacques Paris, was to lie in state for three days, while Orleanians fought in great surging masses to view his frail body and to obtain a scrap of his serge cassock.

The New Orleans of 1819 was still much more French-Spanish than it was American. It had been part of the United States for sixteen years, but changes had not come quickly. The languages heard in the streets were still French and Creole, and the newcomers—the Americans—were still looked upon as barbarians. Though the city was spreading, its heart was still the Place d'Armes before the old Cabildo and the Cathedral. Almost around the corner the notorious Quadroon Balls were at their height of popularity. Duels were still commonplace. Indian squaws sold herbs and baskets in the French Market. People still talked of the pirate-hero, Jean Lafitte.

Marie Laveau was a mixture of Negro, Indian and white bloods. She is described as a tall, statuesque woman with curling black hair, "good" features, dark skin that had a distinctly reddish cast, and fierce black eyes. Both she and Jacques Paris were free people of color. Newspaper reporters later wrote of her father as having been a wealthy white planter, of her mother as a mulatto with a strain of Indian, and though these accounts may not have been accurate, the racial mixture sounds logical. Paris was a quadroon—or three-fourths white—and was one of the Santo Domingo immigrants, according to all indications.

Voodoo was thriving in New Orleans at the time of the Laveau-Paris marriage. The ceremonies near Bayou St. John and Lake Pontchartrain were taking place and the Congo Square dances were Sunday afternoon diversions. The queen was Sanité Dédé, and Marie Saloppé was coming into power. Marie undoubtedly knew all about this, but there is no evidence that she and Jacques were Voodoos. They seem to have been humble and obscure colored people—he was a carpenter by trade. Both were Roman Catholics; it is said Marie was a daily worshipper at the St. Louis Cathedral and sometimes assisted old Père Antoine when he went to nurse yellow-fever victims. The newly married couple lived in what is now the 1900 block of North Rampart Street, in a house given to Marie by her father, Charles Laveau, as a part of her dowry.

Then something happened. They had been married but a short while when Jacques vanished from Marie's life. There is a record of his death some five or six years after the wedding, but long before that Marie was calling herself the "Widow Paris," after the fashion of the period.

It was at this time that Marie began to enter the homes of white people of the city as a hairdresser. In those pre-beauty-parlor days ladies habitually called in a professional hairdresser to arrange their coiffures for important social engagements, and in the New Orleans of that day the profession was usually followed by just such free women of color as Marie. In her

case, this may almost be said to have been the foundation of
her later career as a Voodooienne, for it was now that she
began to learn things that would be to her profit later. As
her deft hands arranged the dark tresses of some Creole ma-
tron, that lady was very likely to talk about herself and her
most intimate affairs in a way she would have talked to no one
else except her priest. Women still confess to their beauticians.

This was not an Anglo-Saxon world. Creole society was
complex and sophisticated, and the individual Creole was no
puritan. When the Americans came the Creoles shocked them
with conduct and a constant seeking after pleasure that was
considered somewhat reprehensible in New England.

Marie must have learned some amazing things. She probably discovered that many Creole marriages were purely business arrangements. She undoubtedly learned that Creole gentlemen almost invariably kept beautiful quadroon mistresses
in cozy little cottages not far from Congo Square. She must
have met grand ladies, who though they presided in their
French opera boxes like duchesses and appeared with their
husbands at great balls and certain *soirées*, spent much of
their time weeping in their boudoirs, or in giving way to
secret alcoholism. All the family skeletons must have come
out to dance for Marie: the family with a strain of insanity
and the strange aunt kept locked in a room upstairs; the public
officials who were stealing the public funds; the family that
was always in fear of someone discovering its strain of Negro
blood. The ladies talked and Marie listened.

How much of this she ever used no one knows, but no
doubt some of it was invaluable. Some she may have shared
with Doctor John in her neophyte days. He was then at his
height, and it is known that they were working together,
at least for a while. She may have learned much from
him.

But Marie's life was not all work. She was a pretty woman,

and men liked her. Just a few years after her separation from Paris one Louis Christophe Duminy de Glapion took up residence in her home and remained there until he died in 1835. Glapion, like Jacques Paris, was a quadroon from Santo Domingo and had fought in the Battle of New Orleans. Of this relationship little can be learned except that Marie bore him fifteen children in rapid succession and retained his affection until his death.

It was after taking Glapion as a lover that Marie Laveau began to be a leader among the Voodoos. By 1830 she was a queen.

There were then many queens. The cult was not well organized. Marie, intelligent, shrewd and an excellent showman, with a strong business sense, seems to have recognized the possibilities in the situation, and she brought into her new profession a rather ruthless talent for doing things thoroughly. Voodoo, for the first time, except for the witch doctor practice of John Bayou, was to be put on a paying basis.

Marie never lessened in any way the mysticism and sensuality of the fanatic Zombi worshippers—all the orthodox trappings of the spectacle were retained: the snake, the black cat, the roosters, the blood-drinking and the finale of fornication—but she added some new tricks, both borrowed and original, principally Roman Catholic statues of saints, prayers, incense and holy water. The Voodoos had been devil-worshippers originally. Marie renounced this and always insisted that her people were Christians. She offered Voodoo to God. Castellanos, in *New Orleans As It Was*, wrote: "To idolatry she added blasphemy. . . ."

The rival queens were quickly disposed of, sometimes with threats, sometimes, it is said, because she used such powerful *gris-gris* against them that they either died or left the city, sometimes by pure brute force, when she met them on the street and beat them soundly until she extracted a promise from them that they would abdicate their thrones or serve under her as sort of sub-queens.

Now the rites by the lake grew not only in size but also in popularity. Marie extended invitations to many persons who had never witnessed the rites; she dismissed much of the secrecy regarding them, as being unnecessary. There were always, it is true, certain meetings to which outsiders were not invited and which they could never have found, but to the usual gatherings Marie invited the press, the police, the sporting world and any thrill-seekers ready to donate a fee for admission. There were other hidden orgies to which white men with a liking for colored girls were welcome. The police did not attend these.

At last she also took charge of Congo Square, and when the white spectators came to watch their slaves dance the Calinda on Sunday afternoons Marie Laveau was presiding over the gathering.

It is scarcely possible that any living person can remember this Marie Laveau. Most old Negroes claim they do, but it is usually not the Widow Paris they describe, although it is extremely difficult to separate mother from daughter. However, Tom Bragg, who is about ninety-five and was born a slave, claims to have seen the first Marie in Congo Square when he was about six years old.

"It was her all right," Tom insisted. "Me, I knows what I'm sayin' 'cause I heared people say she had been married to Mr. Glapion, and she wasn't so young then. She come walkin' into Congo Square wit' her head up in the air like a queen. Her skirts swished when she walked and everybody step back to let her pass. All the people—white and colored—start sayin' that's the most *powerful* woman there is. They say, 'There goes Marie Laveau!' and, me, I was little and I got kind of scared. You know they used to scare little children then by tellin' 'em they was gonna give 'em to Marie Laveau.

"Now let me tell you this. She was a great person. I don't care what nobody says. They had four gates at the Square then, set in a big fence, and at every gate there was four policemens. Sometimes them policemens tried to keep Marie Laveau out, but she jest hypnotized 'em and walked in. She could do that to anybody what got in her way. I seen her make polices git down and bark like dogs.

"Well, when she got in the middle of the Square she took her snake out of a box and danced wit' it. They said she fed that snake on babies, but I ain't sure about that. When she got through dancin' all the other folks would dance—not before. I tell you, she could make anybody do anything and sometimes she made 'em do terrible things. She did most of her work wit' white people, too. She made people disappear. She made wives turn on their husbands and run off wit' other men. She made fine white ladies lie on the ground and roll their bellies."

Josephine Green, an octogenarian, recalled her mother's stories about Marie Laveau.

"My ma seen her," Josephine boasted. "It was back before the war what they had here wit' the Northerners. My ma heard a noise on Frenchman Street where she lived at and she start to go outside. Her pa say, 'Where you goin'? Stay in the house!' She say, 'Marie Laveau is comin' and I gotta see her.' She went outside and here come Marie Laveau wit' a big crowd of people followin' her. My ma say that woman used to strut like she owned the city, and she was tall and good-lookin' and wore her hair hangin' down her back. She looked just like a Indian or one of them gypsy ladies. She wore big full skirts and lots of jewelry hangin' all over her. All the people wit' her was hollerin' and screamin', 'We is goin' to see Papa Limba! We is goin' to see Papa Limba!' My grandpa go runnin' after my ma then, yellin' at her, 'You

come on in here, Eunice! Don't you know Papa Limba is
the devil?' But after that my ma find out Papa Limba meant
St. Peter, and her pa was jest foolin' her."

The Widow Paris thrived on publicity. Legend after legend
spread about her and she seems to have enjoyed them all.
And she had no fear of the law. Charge after charge was
brought against her, but few of them even reached the courts.
The police attended her rites, and in some way she conquered
them. Rumors spread that politicians and city officials were
in her pay. Other rumors whispered that she had learned too
much about the prominent of the city in her hairdresser days.
It is possible both were true. She was in one way or another
collecting on her knowledge. She let the gossip have its way.
She was untouchable.

The most important of her Voodoo work was conducted
from her new home, acquired about 1830, and it has been
substantiated that she used *gris-gris* even in obtaining this. A
young man of wealthy and prominent family had been arrested in connection with a crime, and the evidence against
him is supposed to have been very strong. His father, despair-
ing of proving his innocence, came to Marie, offering to
reward her handsomely for her aid. The day of the trial the
sorceress entered the St. Louis Cathedral at dawn and knelt
at the altar rail for several hours, three Guinea peppers in her
mouth. Then she crept into the Cabildo next door and deposited the peppers under the judge's chair. The youth was dismissed and the happy father presented Marie with a small
cottage on St. Ann Street between North Rampart and Burgundy Streets, almost adjacent to Congo Square. There Marie
Laveau was to live until her death.

That combination of *gris-gris*—the Guinea peppers in her
mouth and prayer at the Cathedral—was typical of the Laveau
practices, which were always a strange commingling of
Voodooism and Catholicism.

Soon the St. Ann Street cottage was as famous as its mistress. It was a low structure set behind a high fence, which almost, though not quite, concealed it from the *banquette*. There was a sloping red-tile roof, a front yard filled with banana trees and bamboo, and a large rear yard containing another small building—probably the kitchen. The section was that in which were located the "little houses" of the quadroon girls and their white lovers, and no doubt this house had served that purpose. However, it pleased Marie to boast that the house was one of the oldest in the city and that it had been in the Laveau family for seven generations, and these absurd pretensions were not only believed by the Negroes around her, but—after a few years—were accepted by a number of whites, even by the newspapers.

Death came to Christophe Glapion in that cottage. The following notice appeared in the *Times* on June 27, 1835:

> Died yesterday, at one o'clock, at the age of 66 years
>
> CHRISTOPHE DUMINY GLAPION
>
> His friends and acquaintances are invited to attend his funeral, without any other invitation, which will take place this evening at precisely five o'clock. The funeral will leave from his home, St. Ann between Burgundy and Rampart Streets.

Marie Laveau was already well known, and great crowds came to Glapion's funeral. The house was always filled with clients. Here Marie sold her *gris-gris*, placed and removed curses, and told fortunes. All afternoon and long after dark each day the people came. Her skill at mind reading was thought remarkable. She knew so many secrets, some learned during her hairdressing days, others still being acquired, for like Doctor John she had her agents planted in many important households throughout the city.

Her control over the Negroes became almost absolute, and

she had more than one way of acquiring this. She would go out late at night and leave a small doll stuck with pins or a wax ball covered with feathers on the stoop of some colored woman in the neighborhood. The next day the terrified creature would arrive at the St. Ann Street house in a frenzy, begging for help and to be "uncrossed." As often as not the person she had chosen was a servant in some wealthy home, and Marie's price would be not money, but a pledge that this servant would serve her as a spy.

Before long her reputation for wisdom and magical powers had spread so that prominent businessmen and city officials were seeking her advice. How much influence the Widow Paris exercised over the city's politicians during that period can never be estimated, but certainly it was very extensive. It is known that for years the most notable attorney in New Orleans was in her employ, and she is said to have advised him as much as he advised her.

Creole ladies came to her, of course, usually in regard to *affaires d'amour*, and carried away her love powders, amulets and other *gris-gris*. Castellanos complains:

Her apartments were often thronged with visitors from every class and section, in search of aid from her supposed supernatural powers. Ladies of high social position would frequently pay her high prices for amulets supposed to bring good luck. Politicians and candidates for office were known to purchase what we would call mascots today at her shop of Fortune, and sports would wear, attached to their watch chains, pieces of bone or wood dug from the graveyard. Some of these were curiously and fantastically carved . . . money poured into her purse.

But all this was only one phase of Marie's activities. There were many angles and for different groups of people there were different Marie Laveaus.

# 8
# Sometimes She
# Danced with a Fish

THERE were frequent meetings at night in the back yard of the St. Ann Street house, and white people did not often see these. Gerald July, a mulatto porter in a New Orleans office building, recalled stories of them that his grandfather had told him.

"They used to meet there every Friday night," he said. "My grandpa would crawl up on the back fence to watch 'em. He was a little kid and they didn't do him nothin'. A white sheet was spread out on the ground, and lighted candles was stuck up all around the edge of it, and in the middle was about five empty bottles. All the dancers, men and women, was naked. The first thing they did was to dance around on the sheet wit' bottles of whiskey and rum in their hands, sprinklin' the sheet wit' liquor and throwin' it on each other. Then they would begin to do another kind of dance, crossin' hands from one side to the other, and all the time singin' them Creole songs. Marie Laveau used to stand in the middle, and she was the only one wit' clothes on. She always wore a long blue dress wit' a full skirt that reached to her ankles. Sometimes she had her hair loose and hangin' down her back, and sometimes she wore a kerchief tied wit' seven knots and the points stickin' straight up. It was what they used to call a *tignon*. She always wore gold hoop earrings, and big gold bracelets on her arms.

"She would call the numbers—you know what I mean? She would tell the dancers what to do and holler all kinds of funny things. Sometimes she'd take a mouthful of whiskey and blow it in somebody's face. My grandpa said that she would call her snake and make it crawl all over the dancers' legs. That snake lived in her yard and it was twenty feet long. I know that's true, because he saw it lots of times. She had a watermelon vine, and she fed the snake on watermelons.

"When the dance got faster the people would holler all kinds of things. They'd go 'Whew! Whew!' and blow more whiskey on each other. They'd keep bobbing up and down and throwing their legs over the candles and the bottles. They would turn around so fast that they'd get dizzy and fall down. Somebody'd throw some whiskey on 'em and they'd be up again. Marie Laveau had a dance she did all by herself. She would wrap that snake around her shoulders and she'd shake and twist herself like she was a snake. Her feet would never move. She had another dance she did wit' a fish. She'd hold a big red fish behind her head and do her snake dance. My grandpa said that was something to see."

Gerald July was certain there were two women called Marie Laveau. "My grandpa said the one he knew best was named Glapion and she was around after he grew up. The one that did them dances in the back yard of her house was her mother. The mother had about fifteen children and one of them, named Marie, took her place as a hoodoo queen. She was a terrible woman—worse than the first. My grandpa went to the funeral when the first Marie Laveau died. He said the newspapers called her the Widow Paris, but she had married Glapion. She had a grown son she called Paris Glapion. Some of the other children died, but some lived a long time and they have children and gran'children livin' right here in New Orleans today."

A white woman living in what is called "downtown" New Orleans also had heard stories from her forebears about what went on in and about the St. Ann Street cottage.

"My mother lived near there when she was small," she said, "and, child, let me tell you she was never allowed to even pass that place. That Voodoo woman kept snakes and black cats, spiders and trained roosters and all sorts of other awful living creatures in that house. She did horrible things. She used to charm people and make 'em die. I know people don't believe that now, but it happened, and everybody in New Orleans knew it at the time. Pregnant women used to go see her and she'd get 'em out of trouble just by burning some candles and saying certain prayers.

"She had a snake she called 'Zombi.' It was her god, and it could do things that brought sickness or health, good luck or bad luck, life or death. There was one rich family my mother knew who had a daughter who wanted to marry a man they didn't like. They went to Marie Laveau and paid her a lot of money and she promised to break up the affair. She took four pigeons and got 'em drunk and she wrote four letters and put one in each of the poor drunk pigeons' mouths. They flew away God knows where, and that boy and girl never did get married. Oh, she was an evil woman!

"My grandmother and grandfather had a two-story house and sometimes after they were asleep my mother would sneak up in the back room. She could look right down into Marie Laveau's back yard. She saw terrible things. They weren't decent, so she would never tell me what they were. She went to her grave with that knowledge. Right now when I go to my husband's tomb I won't pass where Marie Laveau is buried. No, sir!

"I don't know anything about there being two of them. This was nearly a hundred years ago when my mother saw those things; I know that. I'm nearly eighty, so you can figure it out. I lost my husband last spring and when I buried him that was the first time I had thought of that Marie Laveau in years."

By the 1850's Voodoo was at its height in the city, and Marie Laveau was its essence. It is probable that nearly all Negro servants had some connection with the cult. No event in any household in New Orleans was a secret from Marie Laveau. In *Fabulous New Orleans* Lyle Saxon described the grapevine that existed between them:

A message could be conveyed from one end of the city to another in a single day without one white person's being aware of it. It is said that a Negro cook in a kitchen would sing some Creole song while she rattled her pots and pans, a song which sounded innocuous enough to any white listener, but at the end of the verse she would sing a few words intended as a message. Another Negro working near-by would listen intently and at the end of the second verse would hear the message repeated. This second servant would then go outside to attend to her duties. She would sing the same song and her voice would be heard by servants in the house next door. In this way, by means of a song, news of the meeting of a Voodoo society would be carried from one end of the city to another and upon the appointed night Negro men and women would slip from their beds before midnight and would assemble for their ceremonies.

Although the St. John's Eve gatherings near the lake and Bayou St. John became, under Marie's direction, a little like "shows" staged for the benefit of the curious whites, particularly the police and the newspaper reporters, they were by no means anemic affairs. Indeed, the visitors were usually shocked at what took place. The snake in the box was always present, the great caldron steamed upon a roaring bonfire and the Voodoos, the men stripped to loin cloths, the women clad in the loose one-piece garments known as "Mother Hubbards," imbibed quantities of *tafia*, a crude alcoholic drink distilled from molasses. Intoxicated with both the rum and the fanaticism of snake worship, they would form a ring and begin their traditional dances at a signal from their queen, who sometimes stood upon the box containing the snake, sometimes occupied a thronelike chair in the middle of the circle. Music was provided by an aged Negro who scraped a fiddle, said to have been covered with snakeskin, and by drums made of gourds and wine casks over which cowhide had been stretched. As the music grew wilder and the effects of the *tafia* became intensified the dancers were overcome with spasmodic jerking and trembling. Some would whirl in circles until they fell to the ground unconscious; others, with wild screams of frenzy, would run out into the water. The white visitors would usually depart as the climax of sexual orgy began.

But there were still other affairs arranged and conducted by Marie Laveau. She built a house near Milneburg and this she used for several purposes. There, for a fee, she would arrange appointments for white men with mulatto or quadroon girls. This was really carried to its epitome of notoriety by Marie II, but certainly Marie I started it.

The house is variously described as having been a six-room affair, with a hall dividing three rooms on each side, and as a simple one-room shack. It was whitewashed on the outside and was known as the "Maison Blanche." Besides its role as a house of assignation, the Maison Blanche was undoubtedly the scene of some of the Voodoo rites from which non-members were excluded.

Castellanos, after terming the more public rites "a mere device to hoodwink the unwary," writes of the Maison Blanche: "Here secret conclaves were held in a retired spot upon the lake shore known as the *figuiers*—once a big orchard —beyond which she had constructed a frame cabin, that she used as a summer resort."

Alexander Augustin remembered some of the tales of old people which dated to the era of the Widow Paris.

"They would thank St. John for not meddlin' wit' the powers the devil gave 'em," he said. "They had one funny way of doin' this when they all stood up to their knees in the water and threw food in the middle of 'em. You see, they always stood in a big circle. Then they would hold hands and sing. The food was for Papa La Bas, who was the devil. Oldtime Voodoos always talked about Papa La Bas. I heard lots about the Maison Blanche. It was painted white and was built right near the water wit' bushes all around it so nobody couldn't see it from the road. It was a kind of hoodoo headquarters."

It seems to have been only in the Maison Blanche that Marie Laveau would depart from her modernization of the ceremonies and allow the devotees to return to the ways of the immigrants from Santo Domingo. Here, lips smeared with the blood of freshly slaughtered animals and fowl, they took their terrible oaths. Here was the snake, and here the breast was torn from a living chicken and presented to the queen. Here they sang:

> Eh, yé, yé Mamzelle Marie,
> Ya, yé, yé, li konin tou, gris-gris;
> Li té kouri lekal, aver vieux kokodril;
> Oh, ouai, yé Mamzelle Marie. . . .

This was the Marie Laveau who consorted with the crocodiles, the Marie Laveau who talked with Lucifer.

An old man named Pedro, who said he was half Negro, half Mexican, told of having heard of these ceremonies all his life. The participants, he said, would "hiss and crawl on the ground like snakes, hop around croakin' like frogs, creep along, twistin' and shakin' like alligators, screech like hoot owls. I been told they would run around on all-fours, bitin' each other on the legs like they was mad dogs. Some of 'em would dance wit' torches in their hands and there was big bonfires all around the house and up and down the edge of the water. The beach was red like blood all night long."

# 9
# She Brought Them Gumbo and a Coffin

The following small item appeared in the *Daily Picayune* of July 3, 1850:

### CURIOUS CHARGE OF SWINDLING

Marie Laveaux, otherwise Widow Paris, f.w.c., the head of the Voudou women, yesterday appeared before Recorder Seuzeneau and charged Watchman Abreou with having by fraud come into possession of a statue of a virgin, worth $50. We saw the thing called a "statue"; it is a bad looking rag baby, worth about four dimes.

This was the first of several instances in which the Widow Paris sought aid from the courts. She won this case and got her "virgin," even if the court and the reporter did not appreciate its value.

On August 12 of the same year the *Weekly Delta* published a story entitled "The Virgin of the Voudous," but apparently referring to another object. Marie Laveau was not mentioned by name, but certainly she was involved. It seemed the police raided a Voodoo celebration and carried off an object described as "a quaintly carved wooden figure, resembling something between a centaur and an Egyptian mummy." Finally a claimant, described as "a young quadroon" (she may have been Marie II) appeared and was given the image for payment of costs of court—$8.50. As soon as she had gone other Voodoo women tried to claim the idol, until the police were so besieged by them that, according to the newspaper, they began to wonder if they should not have "set it up at auction and knocked it down to the highest bidder." Later some of these women sued, "represented by able counsel," but the court decided that "the holder of the virgin had a right to retain it."

Marie once had trouble with a rival over an idol that may have been the one mentioned. One Rosalie, a quadroon, was attempting to set herself up as an independent Voodoo queen and was actually winning some of Marie's people to her side. Rosalie's main attraction was a large doll carved from wood and painted in brilliant colors and garbed in an elaborate costume of beads and feathers. The new queen claimed to have imported this idol from Africa and that it was a god. Marie, however, solved this problem with her customary way of cutting corners. She simply walked into Rosalie's house one day, when the would-be queen wasn't home, and stole the god, adding it to her own attractions. Rosalie had her arrested, but Marie "proved" to the court that the doll was hers. Marie never lost a case. Nothing more was ever heard of Rosalie.

It is in the early 1850's that the Widow Paris seems to have become interested in prisoners. This soon revealed another facet of her character. Previously, during a yellow fever epidemic, she had gone about nursing the sick, which had given her a reputation for being in reality a very kind woman. Here there is the greatest inconsistency; among some groups she was that "awful old Voodoo," while to others she was an angel of mercy!

There is no record of how visits to the Parish Prison began, but she became a well known figure there, particularly among the men waiting for their executions—the condemned murderers. There is evidence here of her influence with the authorities, for she walked in and out the prison as if she owned it, spent long hours with the men in their dismal cells; she donated an altar to the chapel within the prison and decorated and cared for it with her own hands. Most curious of all is the fact that neither in the chapel nor in any of her work among the prisoners was there any outward indication of Voodooism. This Marie Laveau was a devout and earnest Roman Catholic, at least so far as appearances were concerned.

The first publicity this part of her activities received was in 1852, when Jean Adam and Anthony Deslisle were condemned to die for the murder of a young mulatto servant girl. The girl had been alone in the house of her mistress, Madame Chevillon, when the two men, house painters by trade, had entered it one Sunday morning, cut her throat and stolen a large sum of money they had known Madame kept in her home. They were arrested, after the case had caused considerable excitement in the city, and were tried and condemned to be hanged.

Marie came to see the men every day while they awaited execution. Each morning she brought them food, talked with them and knelt with them in prayer. The last morning she brought them gumbo and remained with them until almost the very hour of execution. Then she departed to join the crowd outside. All New Orleans executions were then public.

When the men appeared they were both in an obvious state of intoxication. Deslisle was roaring drunk and Adam was almost unconscious and had to be carried to the platform where the gallows was situated. Hundreds of Orleanians were gathered in Orleans Street to see the execution. The day was bright and sunny, with a cloudless sky overhead, and many people had brought their children. It was an occasion for which hundreds had waited anxiously since the occurrence of the terrible crime.

Immediately upon his appearance Deslisle began a wild harangue, shouting at the spectators that he was innocent and begging them to attend his funeral and to see that he had a fine one with a long procession. Then he would cry that he was a Frenchman and would die only for the French flag and not for these barbarous Americans. Then, as he reached the platform, he raised his arms upward, stared toward the sky and uttered a terrified scream. The crowd gazed upward and saw a cloud like a black cape hovering above the gallows. Deslisle screamed again and fainted into the arms of the guards.

A moment later the whole sky was nearly black. What had been a blue-and-gold morning became a gray twilight. There was a dull roar of wind and the trees in the vicinity swayed and groaned. Children began to cry. A woman in the crowd shouted, "It's just like the Crucifixion!" and swooned.

The execution went on as scheduled. Their arms bound, the murderers were placed in chairs on the platform, their heads were covered with the black hoods and the twin loops were placed around their necks. The sheriff raised his hand and the executioner sprung the trap. As this happened rain came down in torrents and the dark sky was shattered by lightning. The newspaper account of it all next day said it was as if "the floodgates of the heavens were opened to deluge the world again."

Then a thrill of horror passed through the watching mob. They saw the sheriff and other officials rush to the opening and look down. The ropes which should have been taut hung loosely and swayed in the wind. The nooses had slipped over the heads of the men and they were sprawled on the pavement below, Deslisle trying to crawl about on his hands and knees, his right arm broken, blood streaming over his face and childish sobs coming from his lips. Adam lay unconscious, bleeding from a wound in his skull. The crowd surged forward and the police had to use their clubs.

The men were carried into the prison, but ten minutes later were dragged back to the platform and were hanged, this time successfully. A few minutes later the storm subsided, vanished, and the sun came back into the sky. A tall woman in a *tignon* moved away from those spectators who had remained, impervious to the whispers, "There goes Marie Laveau!"

It was Marie Laveau they talked about a long time afterward, whenever the Deslisle-Adam case was mentioned. Thousands of Orleanians were convinced that she had caused the storm and that she had tried, almost successfully, to save the lives of the two men. And because of this case the Louisiana Legislature met and forever outlawed public executions.

They say that she once did cheat the gallows of a victim. Antoine Cambre was of an old and distinguished Creole family, but had led an erratic existence, spending most of his time drinking and carousing. One night very late he had an argument with a lamplighter in one of the city's streets and in a drunken rage shot and killed the old man. After a long trial he was sentenced to be hanged, and Marie Laveau began the usual visits to the death cell. Castellanos hinted at a former friendship, saying, "It was usual . . . to allow prisoners about to suffer death . . . to erect an altar. This altar was placed in the hands of Marie Laveau, who, from her previous intimacy with Cambre, was thought to be the proper person."

The day before the execution Marie is supposed to have asked him, "My young one, before you die, tell me what you want to eat." The man shook his head sullenly, too miserable to think of eating. "I'll make you a gumbo such as you have never eaten in your whole life," the Voodooienne is said to have promised. When the guards came for the condemned man the next day they found him on the floor, writhing in his last agony. He had eaten Marie Laveau's gumbo.

In 1859 Marie achieved notoriety when she brought James Mullen his coffin. They worked together day after day, decorating the coffin inside and out with religious pictures. At night Mullen slept in the casket, using the dress of his three-year-old daughter as a pillow, and every day Marie prayed with him, until he was hanged.

The same year the Voodoo queen worked with a trio of murderers, Heinrich Haas, Peter Smith and Joseph Linsay. Haas seems to have received most of her attention and with her assistance he decorated the walls and ceilings with pictures of a religious nature.

As late as 1868 she was a constant visitor to the cell of Joseph Bazar, who had beaten his wife's lover to death with a large stone. When Bazar stood at the gallows with the noose around his neck a messenger on horseback galloped into the prison yard, bearing a commutation of sentence from Governor Warmouth. That time Marie Laveau seems to have done her work well.

She was growing old now, though she still had long years of life ahead of her. It is recorded that in 1869 she reigned as queen over a Voodoo conclave for the last time. On March 21 of that year the *New Orleans Times* told how—

At one end of the chapel a corpse was exposed. The rites having been commenced, an elderly turbaned female dressed in yellow and red (Marie Laveau), ascended a sort of dais and chanted a wild fetish song, to which the others kept up an accompaniment with their voices and with a drumlike beat of their hands and feet. At the same time they commenced to move in a circle, while gradually increasing their time. As the motion gained in intensity the flowers and other ornaments disappeared from their hair, and their dresses were torn open, and each one conducted herself like a bacchante. Everyone was becoming drunk and intoxicated with the prevailing madness and excitement. As they danced in a circle, in the center of which stood a basket with a dozen hissing snakes whose heads were projecting from the cover, each *corybante* touched a serpent's head with her brand. . . .

Two months later, on June 7, 1869, the cult held a meeting and reached a decision that since Marie Laveau was now past seventy she should be retired.

However, this retirement meant little more than that she would no longer preside over the rites and dances. She was still the dominant figure in the Voodoo world and her house remained a magnet for thousands. This was to continue for some years. The Widow Paris was not yet ready to die.

Two years after her abdication a piece in the *Daily Picayune* offered proof that her prison work was continuing. On May 10, 1871, the newspaper reported that:

Yesterday the reporter visited the condemned cells of Pedro Abriel and Vincent Bayume, appointed to suffer death on the 13 inst. Since Sunday the preparations for their execution have been going steadily on. The prison has been put in a state of complete renovation, and wears an almost holiday appearance. The halls are white, and the casings and iron railings have been newly painted. But this is not the chief feature of interest. This is the condemned cell.

For more than twenty years, whenever a human being has suffered the final penalty in the Parish Prison, an old colored woman has come to their cell and prepared an altar for them. This woman is Marie Laveau, better known as a priestess of the Voudous. Arriving at the prison yesterday morning, she proceeded at once to prepare an altar for the worship of the men who have been sentenced to expiate the guilt of murder on the scaffold. . . .

It was 1875 when Marie entered her home in St. Ann Street, and she did not leave it again until her death six years later. It was then that the strangest part of the entire Laveau mystery became most noticeable. For Marie Laveau still walked the streets of New Orleans, a new Marie Laveau, who also lived in the St. Ann Street cottage. Not that this began with the retirement of Marie I. It had begun some years before, when a younger woman had been pointed out as the ruler of the Voodoos.

Now a passerby sometimes told of having seen a withered crone with yellow skin and wisps of white hair showing from beneath a dingy *tignon* and announced he had seen "Marie Laveau's mother." The neighborhood and the generations were changing, and though people were well aware of the existence of Marie Laveau, they were forgetting the Widow Paris.

# 10
# They All Danced
# Naked as Jaybirds

NO one knows when the daughter first took the place of the mother and became "Marie Laveau." It seems there was no definite date when the transition took place, but rather that there was an occasional substitution at first, later a complete one. Stories of the youth and beauty of "Marie Laveau" late in the 1850's are the earliest indications of the substitution. The Widow Paris was then well past middle age. Yet Marie II understudied the role so successfully that all New Orleans historians have confused the two.

This other Marie was born on February 2, 1827, to Marie I and Christophe Glapion. Nothing is known of her early life. She was one of the many Glapion children inhabiting the St. Ann Street cottage, and why or when her mother chose her for the role she was to play—or whether she chose it for herself—remains a mystery. In any case, as Tony Miller, inmate in a home for the aged colored people of New Orleans, said, "The daughter lived her mother again."

Like her mother she was beautiful. There seems to have been a remarkable resemblance between them. This Marie Laveau was also tall and very straight. She had thick black hair that curled but slightly, a thin, straight nose and sensual lips. Her eyes were large, very black and rather startling. (There is the additional legend that their pupils were shaped like half-moons!) Her skin was smooth and her coloring somewhere between bronze and peach; she was probably lighter than her mother. Writers of the era tell of a "Vol-

tairian look," a severe and penetrating expression invaluable
to nurses of children, who had only to threaten to "give
them to Marie Laveau," to curb any brewing disobedience.

This is the Marie Laveau old people usually remember.
She inspired far more fear than the first. Half a legend, for
some of this awe was based on tales of events that had actually
occurred in relation to the Widow Paris, rather than to herself, she does seem to have been a sterner personality. Her
prison work and her nursing of the yellow-fever victims
revealed a warm core in Marie I; there is little indication of
this in Marie II.

"She was a great woman," said old Tony. "She was sure
hard-boiled and she liked the money, but she was great. When
I remember her it was around 1870 and she was about forty
years old, but looked younger. She was light and could have
passed for a Spanish lady. She was big and well built, and
the mens used to go kind of crazy lookin' at her. She had
the reddest lips I ever seen in my life. She wore a *tignon*, wit'
little curls hangin' down around her face, and she always had
big gold hoops in her ears. She wore blue dresses made of
cotton that had big skirts that went to the tops of her shoes,
wit' a waist buttoned straight down the front and come in
tight in the middle; it sure showed off her bust. She always
wore long sleeves that puffed out at the shoulders, and there
was buttons down the front of her skirt. I can see her now
and if I was an artist I could paint her for you. She walked
just like a queen."

Tony knew nothing of Marie I. "I ain't never heared of
no other Marie Laveau," he said. "There was a crowd of
people livin' in that house on St. Ann, but I never did know
who they all was."

The house had become crowded by the time Marie II was
grown. Marie I had borne Glapion fifteen children and,
though some of these had died, there were grandchildren of

various ages, sizes, and shades of color. There are accounts of the construction of an addition to the house; no doubt it was needed. Some of the children vanished completely—one daughter is said to have "married a white man and gone North"—nevertheless each year the household grew.

Like her mother, Marie II began her career as a hairdresser. During one period she left the family cottage and opened some sort of a hairdressing establishment, the location of which is designated as having been "on Royal Street down toward Esplanade." During another period she operated a place in Bourbon Street between Toulouse Street and St. Peter Street. The house is believed to be the first one in the block from Toulouse Street, on what Orleanians call "the river side," and had been the slave quarters of the house facing Toulouse, now a bar. It is still there. She had living quarters above the downstairs place of business and here she told fortunes and sold *gris-gris*. Later she returned to the Laveau household.

Raoul Desfrene, a "French Negro" of 77, remembered Marie II well and attended some of her rites when he was a boy of about fourteen. What impressed him most was the jewelry he said she wore, which included, besides the ponderous gold earrings, diamond and ruby clasps in her scarlet-and-blue *tignons*, many rings set with diamonds and other precious stones, a huge horseshoe brooch of diamonds and a heavy gold bracelet on each arm. "She sure used to dress up," he said.

He dismissed Marie I with, "There was an old lady living there, but nobody paid her no mind." Raoul enjoyed describing the home of the Laveaus. According to him there was an altar for "good luck and good work" in the front room. It was covered with a white cloth and held a statue of the Virgin and one of Saint Peter. Raoul recalled one of another saint, a Saint Marron, who, he explained, "was a colored saint white people don't know nothing about. Even the priests ain't never heard of him 'cause he's a real hoodoo saint."

But this altar in the front room was secondary to another at the back of the house, Raoul believed. "In the back," he said, "was the altar for bad work. On it was statues of a bear, a tiger, a lion and a wolf. Right in the middle was a big carved box with a snake inside it. That box and snake had been sent to Marie Laveau from Africa and that snake was the devil. I know that's true, 'cause I seen it myself, me."

Every Monday Marie went to the home of a Voodoo woman called Mama Antoine, which was located on Dumaine Street. It was "almost next door" to Raoul's home. "They used to hire me to go over and sing at the meetings," he said. "I used to have a good voice, and I sang at all them Mama Antoine meetings and sometimes at others they had."

The Monday night gatherings were known as *parterres*. A feast was spread for the spirits present, on a white tablecloth laid on the floor. The food included *congris*, apples, oranges and red peppers. There were lighted candles in the four corners of the room; Raoul recalled their colors as red, blue, green and brown. He was certain they never used white. A Negro named Zizi played the accordion and among the women who always did Voodoo dances was Regina Nicaud, who later became a Voodoo queen, and a girl named Georgina Laveau, who was, Raoul thought, either sister, niece or daughter to Marie; even then he had not been clear about the relationship. There was also another woman he remembered as a "good Voodoo," and who was known as "Josephine Bayou."

Raoul could remember some of the gatherings near Lake Pontchartrain during that period. "They did the *Fe Chauffe* dance," he said. "I can't do it now, but it was wild. These was held out on a barge right in the lake sometimes. Seven or eight bottles was placed in a circle and the dancers had to dance around and all in between them. There was lots of little pots of fire all around the edge of the barge. You won't believe it, but them *Fe Chauffe* dancers balanced lighted candles on their heads the whole time they danced and the candle flames never went out. They used to drink lots of rum and champagne and everybody got howling drunk. They was a sight!

"There was a gang of white ladies what had money and they'd pay Marie Laveau ten dollars each to come to them *Fe Chauffe* dances. You'd see 'em come, all dressed up and wearin' thick veils, but when they sent their carriages away, they'd take off their shoes and stockings and all their clothes 'cept their chemises. Then they'd dance on the barges with lighted candles on their heads. Marie Laveau would stand in the middle and shake and sing, and they'd dance around her in a circle. You can't see nothing like that nowadays, no."

Raoul thought the last *Fe Chauffe* dance he saw took place in 1879. Marie I was in her eighties and bedridden.

In so far as reigning as queen of the celebrations on St. John's Eve is concerned Marie II did not often serve in that capacity. The position of the Laveaus had become so lofty in the Voodoo world that neither mother nor daughter was in that late period a mere queen, but rather a sort of "queen of queens," with less important women operating under their guidance. Accordingly, when Marie I was retired in 1869, one Eliza, a quadroon woman, was appointed to reign over the next year's rite. Numerous queens and witch doctors served under the supreme direction of one or the other of the Laveaus.

However, a reporter for the *New Orleans Times* attended the St. John's Eve affair of 1872 and found Marie Laveau (undoubtedly Marie II) presiding. On June 28 an account of the event was published in that paper as follows:

An obliging correspondent who was fortunate enough to reach the scene of the voudous incantation some hours before our reporter, sends us the following graphic description of the earlier portion of the ceremony. . . .

On Monday morning (St. John's Day) I went to the French Market for the express purpose of finding out from an old negress, who sells in the market and whom I have known for years to be well posted—"she is one of them"—the exact spot where the Voudou Festival would be held this year. Knowing that I had attended many of them before, she told me immediately. She made me faithfully promise that I would tell no one.

Thus posted, I took the 8 o'clock train on the Pontchartrain Railroad. Arriving at the lake I fooled around a little; saw great crowds—all looking for the place, but very few, if any, knowing where it would be. I made up my mind not to walk or ride to the scene, so I hired a skiff and pulled to the mouth of Bayou St. John —the best way of getting there from the lake end—the festival took place near Bayou Tchoupitoulas. Upon arriving at the shanty I found congregated about two hundred persons of mixed colors— white, black, and mulattoes. I knew the larger portion of them, and was received with pleasure. The ceremonies had not begun. A few moments after my arrival a large crowd arrived in a lugger, say about one hundred more, making a total of three hundred. Soon there arrived a skiff containing ten persons, among which was the Voudou Queen, Marie Lavaux. She was hailed with hurrahs.

The people were about equally divided male and female—a few more females. The larger portion of the crowd Negroes and quadroons, but about one hundred whites, say thirty or forty men, the remainder women.

Upon the arrival of Marie Lavaux, she made a few remarks in Gumbo French, and ended them by singing, "*Saiya ma coupê ça*, to which all hands joined in the chorus of "*Mamzelle Marie chauffez ça.*"

It was then about eleven o'clock. The song ended, orders were given by the queen to build a fire as near the edge of the lake as possible, which was "did," every one being compelled to furnish a piece of wood for the fire, making a wish as they threw it on. Then a large caldron was put on the fire; it was filled with water brought in a beer barrel; then salt was put in by an old man, who jabbered something in Creole; then black pepper was put in by a young quadroon girl; she sang while putting in the pepper; then a box was brought up to the fire, from which was taken a black snake; he was cut in three pieces (the Trinity), one piece was put in by Marie Lavaux, one piece by the old man who put in the salt, and one piece by the young girl, who put in the pepper; then all joined in chorus of the same song: "*Mamzelle Marie chauffez ça;*" then the queen called for a "cat," it was brought, she cut its throat, and put it into the kettle.

Another repetition of the same chorus, then a black rooster was brought to the queen. She tied its feet and head together and put it in the pot alive. Repetition of the chorus. Then came an order from the queen for every one to undress, which all did, amid songs and yells. The queen then took from her pocket a shot bag full of white and colored powders. She gave orders for every one to join hands and circle around the pot. Then she poured the powders into the pot, sang a verse of some oracle song, to which all joined in a chorus while dancing around the pot, "*C'est l'amour, oui Maman c'est l'amour,* etc."

She then looked at her watch, and shouted *Li minuit tous moune à l'eau*—it is 12 o'clock all hands in the water—and everybody went into the lake, remained in the bath about half an hour. Upon coming out they began singing and dancing for another hour, when all were halted to listen to a speech by the queen. She preached her sermon, ending with, "I give you all half an hour recreation." Then the crowd scattered promiscuously. In half an hour the horn was blown (a sea shell), and all hands hurried back to the queen, and set up another chorus to a verse she sang to the same tune as the first one.

After the song she said "You can now eat," [and] those who brought victuals, such as gumbo, jambalaya, etc., all began eating and drinking until the horn was again blown, when all hurried to the pot, the fire was put out from under it, water thrown on and around it by four nude black women, with white handkerchiefs on their heads. During this time the chorus was kept up of "*Mamzelle Marie Chauffez . . .*" Then the whole contents of the pot was poured back into the same barrel the water was taken from, the queen saying, as this was done, *pour l'année prochaine* (for the next year).

The queen then said: "You must all dress up again," which was "did." The bugle was again sounded, all hands joined around the queen. She preached another sermon, at the close of which all knelt down to pray and receive her benediction. Another chorus of *C'est l'amour, oui Maman c'est l'amour*, during which day began to break. Then the queen said: "Here is day, we must welcome it with song, and all go home." I took my skiff, left them there, pulled to Pontchartrain Railroad, and came back into the city.

This scene seems to have been fairly representative of the spectacles the white people who sought to view a Voodoo gathering were permitted to attend.

Mattie O'Hara, a white woman of Irish extraction, who lived for seventy-one years near the lake front, said that Marie Laveau appeared at several St. John's Eve meetings out there. "It was the only time she come," said the old lady. "Other times she let the other queens hold the dances. My mother told me with her own tongue about how they carried on, and my mother never spoke a word in her life that wasn't God's own truth. On St. John's Eve this whole section was looking like a scene in hell with the fires of their torches and their burning pots and bonfires. My mother never went near them except for three years when her curiosity got the better of her good sense. It was all very immoral. The police would come out sometimes, but she—that Laveau woman—would hoodoo them and they would take off their clothes, too. Can you imagine all them people, white and colored, dancing around like devils, and all of them naked as jaybirds? They would all run out into the water and carry on out there. One man with a big voice would sing, 'Going to go swimming right in St. John's Lake?' And they'd all answer him, and sing, 'Yes, Little John!' "

Mrs. O'Hara made the sign of the Cross. "My mother used to sing that to me sometimes and I'd shiver," she said. "I could feel the devil breathing down my neck. She could do it just like them hoodoos. 'Going to go swimming right in St. John's Lake? Yes, Little John!'

"One of the worst things about that Laveau woman was she could steal anybody's husband from her. I know many a man left his family to try to get next to Marie Laveau. The funny thing was most of the time men couldn't get nowhere with her. They just followed her around like dogs. That was because they was hoodooed. She put a spell on them. She was a wicked, evil woman and she talked to the devil."

Old Voodoos and their descendants remember the "Wishing Spot" near Lake Pontchartrain, a place which seems to have played an important role in the ceremonies conducted by Marie II. Its exact location is now unknown, but it must have once attracted thousands of persons.

According to most of the accounts, to reach the Wishing Spot the devotees crossed Esplanade Street Bridge, then walked about half a mile along the curves of Bayou St. John. Here a particular type of ceremony was performed. The queen, the chosen king and an assistant—often called the "valet"— took positions, the queen in the center, the king on one side, the valet on the other. Each placed the left hand over the heart and stretched the other over the water, and retained that position for some minutes, meditating upon the wishes they desired granted. The devotees would assume similar postures behind the three dignitaries, each also meditating upon his wish. There was a period of perfect silence. The trio would then approach the water, bend low over it and murmur certain secret words in the "unknown tongue," which no one but the three could understand. Then, suddenly, at a signal from the queen, they would all leap into the water, chanting in unison, "*Nous allons mourir dans ce lac, c'est vrai! Nous allons mourir dans ce lac!*" After this, when the drenched cultists emerged, a feast of gumbo and chicken was served. The Voodoos always ate at the conclusion of their ceremonies.

The Wishing Spot appears in no accounts of the Voodoos until 1875, so it was probably the invention of Marie II.

Orleanians visited the Wishing Spot for years, and then at last forgot where it was. Gloria White, a colored schoolteacher, recalled her grandmother's description of the Wishing Spot.

"When I was little my grandmother was always talking about it," she said. "Sometimes she'd go off on mysterious journeys for a whole day and come back to tell us she had made a wish. The strange part is she always got them. I guess she was one of the few old people left who knew where it was. If I had been older I would have made her tell me, but I was too young to think of that then. I know I believed it all then, and when she went off to the Wishing Spot to make her wish it was just like somebody going to a store to buy something. She told us hundreds of people used to believe in it when she was young. They always went on Friday, sometimes at noon, sometimes at three in the afternoon and sometimes at midnight. The Wishing Spot was really an old tree trunk near the edge of the bayou. They would stand there ten rows deep, wishing and praying. Sometimes they bowed down to the tree stump, and they would drop money in it before they left. I guess Marie Laveau made money that way.

"But even after she was gone people kept on going there. One of the things I remember my grandmother saying was that they went in all kinds of weather—even in storms. My grandmother used to say, too, that more white people went than Negroes. I wonder how many people believed in it."

Marie II had many profitable activities. For one thing, she greatly increased the reputation of the name of "Marie

Laveau" as a procuress. Her mother had built the Maison
Blanche and had sometimes arranged meetings between white
men and colored girls. Marie II let it be known that her
services were always available in this particular field of
endeavor.

One white man in downtown New Orleans claimed to have
attended such an affair at the Maison Blanche.

"I'll tell you the truth," he said bluntly, "the way I see it
that place wasn't nothing but a fancy kind of whorehouse,
and Marie Laveau was the Madame. She had some special
tricks going on out there that the young fellows used to like.
You would arrange it in advance by sending somebody to her
house on St. Ann Street. She would fix a date—usually a
Saturday night—to have her gals out there, as many as there
was fellows in the party. It cost a lot because there was plenty
of food and wine and champagne. You had to give ten
dollars for each girl, besides paying for the stuff. Marie
Laveau didn't fool with no pikers.

"The girls all danced with you naked and everybody drank
lots of liquor and got higher 'n hell. After a while, when the
guys got all heated up, the girls would start acting cute and
running away from them. They always fought and carried
on, but whatever gal you caught was yours. Marie Laveau
always sat in a rocking chair in one corner of the room,
saying her beads and watching what was going on. She never
fooled with anybody herself. Of course that was around
1885 and she was about sixty years old."

A restaurateur at a present-day resort near the lake had
heard of the Maison Blanche.

"It was one large room with whitewashed walls inside and
out," he said. "Marie Laveau used to bring nine or ten light-
skinned colored gals out there every Wednesday, Saturday
and Sunday night. No Negro men were allowed, but there
were always a lot of fancy white sports with checkered vests,

and sometimes some of the city politicians. From what I've heard it was just a meeting place. They'd eat and drink some liquor and maybe dance a little, but then they took the girls off in their carriages. There 're so many stories you don't know what went on there exactly, but I don't think it had anything to do with religion."

The stories do vary so much that it is difficult to verify tales about the Maison Blanche. Most, like the above, are merely hearsay. But Pop Abou, who despite his strange name is a meek little Negro in his eighties, with failing eyesight, swears he knows the truth.

"I remembers it like yesterday," said Pop. "A lot of folks sure is mixed up. I knows the truth and I wasn't old and blind then. I been to plenty of Marie Laveau's dances. It's true they was lots of white men and yellow gals at that house. Marie Laveau did that for money. But she never had no food there and she never had no champagne. She was too smart to lose her profits that way. She had beer and wine. The only music they used was a drum made out of a barrel with a piece of skin stretched over it, and she hired a nigger to beat that with his hands.

"But them dances was only a side line with her and they didn't have anything to do with hoodoo. At the real hoodoo dances she had people coming from all over the world. Some of them left her money and that's all she was after. When the polices come messin' around she would holler at 'em, 'Shut that goddam door!' There wasn't no door when they was all out there in the open, but that meant for them to get away because they wasn't wanted. And they used to get out. She could have a policeman fired with one snap of her fingers and she could get one promoted with two snaps. Sometimes she used hoodoo to do that and sometimes she just walked into a big politician's office and said 'Do it! I is Marie Laveau and I wants it done.' And he knew better 'n not to do. If he didn't something awful bad was sure gonna happen to him. That's the truth. A lot of things they say about her is lies, but that is true. You may not believe it, but that woman was the real boss of New Orleans."

# 11
# She Kept Skeletons
# in Her Armoire

BUT the most important Laveau work was still done in the cottage on St. Ann Street. For years, in a back room, old and shrunken, lay—the real, if you like—Marie Laveau, the Widow Paris. Few persons saw her. Some who did were told by Marie II that she was an old woman she had taken in out of pity. Others knew her as "Marie Laveau's mother." Most Negroes had forgotten her and knew only the current Marie.

There was still a constant stream of clients and visitors. New Orleans was growing more American now, and many Creoles were intermarrying with the Anglo-Saxons. The city was becoming cosmopolitan and, in a way, more sophisticated, but some of its color was fading. Those Orleanians who remained fiercely and stubbornly Creole became a minority who secluded themselves from the rest of the population, snubbed the "new society," and refused to live—sometimes even to visit—in the neighborhoods above Canal Street. English was now the language taught in the schools and spoken on the streets. It was the beginning of a new era.

Marie II, however, had no trouble obtaining clients. As many came as had come to her mother, to buy the same *gris-gris* and to listen to the same advice, though all was sold at higher prices.

There were the same rumors, many persons still vowing that she kept a huge snake in her yard—or in her house, or under her bed. There were others who denied the existence of any such reptile. One old man, still living, will take a vow that Marie Laveau was afraid of snakes!

There were the same horror tales and the whispers of human sacrifice; they still persist.

"I lived across the street from her in 1880," Marie Breaux, an old Frenchwoman, will tell you. "She was an evil woman, her. She killed babies that were not wanted by their mothers. She used to hang their bodies up in her chimney like hams and smoke them. Oh, she killed lots of children. They say her *armoire* was filled with skeletons. Me, I moved out of that neighborhood as soon as I found myself living near a woman like that. I still thank God that I am alive. She was awful!"

At least one living man, a Negro undertaker, claims to have once owned one of these mummies.

"We had it in our family for years," he said. "My father bought it from Marie Laveau for twenty dollars. It was coal black and hard as a stone and people used to come from all over to see it. When I got married my wife couldn't stand the sight of it, so to please her I took it out and threw it in the river. People used to tell her that she would never have a baby with that thing in the house, and she wanted to have children. Now we have five."

White families seem to have sometimes lived across the street from the Laveaus. Miss Annie Ferguson had childhood memories of the carriages before the door of the cottage, of veiled ladies who entered and departed, and of terrifying stories of witchcraft.

"Many a morning my father found little dolls and other peculiar things on our front steps," she said. "I think Marie Laveau didn't like us and wanted us to move. And we did. We didn't like it there any better than she liked having us, once we realized what we had across the street from us. I never saw the inside of that house. My mother would have died at the idea of my entering it. But it is true that many society women and prominent men used to go to her for advice. Sometimes they carried home human bones in their pockets. Human bones! It was all so horrible. You never know what people are really like. I remember one other thing. Sometimes a lot of Indians used to sleep in her side yard. They were the kind who sold baskets and herbs in the French Market, you know, and if they missed the last ferry—most of them lived across the river—they'd sleep there. People said Marie Laveau was part Indian and that some of these people were her relatives, but you don't know what to believe. I saw her several times and she looked more Indian than anything else, only she was better looking. But I didn't look at her long. If somebody would say, 'Here comes Marie Laveau!' I'd run inside to my mother. I was that afraid of her."

Miss Ferguson suddenly recalled another fact. "I talked to a colored woman once who went inside that terrible house," she said. "She told me that right in the center of the floor of the front room there was a pan of sugar with drops of fresh blood on top of it!" The old lady concluded with what seems to be proof that her memory was of Marie II: "She was using a false name, too. Lots of people told me her real name was Marie Glapion and that she had taken her mother's name because her mother had been a famous Voodoo queen, too."

The *gris-gris* sold by Marie II included small bags to be worn for protection or for good luck. These were bits of cloth into which were placed such articles as bits of bone, colored pebbles, goofer dust—dirt from a graveyard—some salt and some ground red pepper. Others were more elaborate, one being a tiny nest woven from horsehair and pierced with two crossed roots. These were sewn to the hem of a skirt or to a garter, for the purpose of warding off evil. George W. Cable reported having seen one containing cat hair and dog hair, mixed with salt and pepper. Still others were made of red flannel and contained a lodestone; these were—and still are—considered very helpful to gamblers. Another sort held gunpowder and red pepper; these were powerful *wangas* to be thrown into somebody's path to cause them to get into fights.

Descriptions of these charms sometimes sound ridiculous. One such was of a bag made from a shroud of a person who had been buried nine days. Into this was placed, according to reports, a dried, one-eyed toad, a dried lizard, the little finger of a Negro who had committed suicide, the wings of a bat, the eyes of a cat, the liver of an owl and the heart of a rooster. This was—as it certainly deserved to be—an extremely powerful weapon against evil. If it were placed inside the pillow of an enemy, he would die. That is not difficult to believe, either.

Marie II trained many of her people to prepare *gris-gris*, and it was not unusual for white persons who were unpopular with their servants to find their pillows very uncomfortable. Often someone opening such a pillow, would find that some of the feathers had been arranged in a peculiar fashion—rolled into tight balls or shaped into the form of a rooster and securely tied with twine. This still goes on—and there is never any indication of the pillow having been opened. Lyle Saxon told of opening a pillow for someone, while visiting on a plantation, and finding inside a pecan through which two feathers had been thrust, forming a cross.

Conjure-balls were sold at the Laveau cottage. These were sometimes made of black wax and were supposed to contain a piece of human flesh. Often they were stuck with pins or marked with blood. One of the Laveau instructions was that a conjure ball be rolled across the lawn or yard of an enemy during the night. This would bring about a death or some other misfortune within the household of the enemy.

Gamblers were advised to take a small piece of chamois, another of red flannel, a shark's tooth, sap from a pine tree and blood from a dove. The blood and sap were mixed together, and the amount the gambler wished to win was written upon the chamois with this mixture. The chamois was then covered with the red flannel, with the shark's tooth between the two, and sewn together with cat's hair. This was to be worn in the left shoe. Results were assured, but it must have been uncomfortable.

There was a simple way of making a stingy friend spend his money. Marie II advised the client to bathe in a tub half filled with water into which a box of borax, a box of cinnamon and a teacupful of sugar had been added. Upon meeting this miser, the miser would spend every cent he possessed upon the one who had performed such an ablution.

Sometimes even preachers—though they often denounced her from their pulpits—came to Marie II, desperate because of their waning congregations. She would tell them to buy ammonia, sugar and nutmeg and to use this in the water used to scrub the church. For extreme cases she sometimes recommended that whiskey be thrown into the four corners of the church. It has been reported that churches following her advice always showed an increase in attendance.

There were many ways of winning court cases and of swaying judges and juries. Like her mother, Marie II was expert in this. To have a prisoner released she would sometimes ask for the names of the jury, the judge and the prosecuting attorney. These were written on a piece of paper and the paper was placed into a hole chipped in a large block of ice and covered with powdered sugar. Nine candles were arranged around the block of ice. Then Marie and her client would lie on their backs on the floor before the ice and she would rap nine times with her fist upon the floor, saying certain prayers in Creole and in the "unknown tongue."

Often, after listening to the details of the case, she would decide that the best plan was to make the judge ill. To accomplish this she would melt a black candle, place a piece of paper containing the judge's name inside the wax, knead and roll it into a ball, then place the ball in a tub of water. All of the night before the day of the trial Marie would sit beside the tub, turning the ball with a stick. The judge would not appear in court the next day.

There was an evil *gris-gris* she sold to servants who wanted to get even with their master or mistress for some real or fancied wrong. It consisted of saffron, salt, gunpowder and pulverized dog manure. White persons were constantly finding little sacks of black paper containing this mixture in their homes—in dresser drawers, in kitchen cabinets, perhaps secreted inside the piano. More than one debutante, arriving at a ball, found some such repulsive article inside her handbag, when she opened it to powder her nose. Occasionally she might find a little wax doll stuck with pins, but, despite their frequency in fiction about Voodoo, dolls were rarely used in the practices.

The Laveau ways of performing homeopathic magic were endless. Sick people were often brought to the house to receive the benefit of a cure by Marie II. A person bitten by a snake was told to get another live snake of any sort, cut its head off "while it was angry" and to tie this head to the wound. This was to be left attached until sunrise of the following day. Sometimes her practices contained an element of medical truth, embracing the use of roots and herbs that contained genuine curative elements. For sprains and swellings she used hot water containing Epsom salts and rubbed the injured parts with whiskey, chanting prayers and burning candles at the same time, of course. For other ailments she administered castor oil, to the accompaniment of incantations and prayer.

To make a person change his mind black candles were

burned half an hour, then were melted. The individual's name was written four times backward and five times forward on a scrap of silk paper, put into the wax. This lump was then thrown under his house. Next, his name was written once on another bit of silk paper and the paper was placed in a cocoanut together with honey and sugar. This was to "sweeten" him. The cocoanut was rolled from the front to the back door of the house, while the one rolling it repeated over and over again, "Your head is as hard as a cocoanut, but you're going to change your mind." When Marie II "worked on" a person, she worked thoroughly.

To get rid of a person his name was written on a small balloon, the balloon was tied to a statue of St. Expédite, and then was released into the air. The person would depart in whatever direction the balloon was carried by the wind.

Marie II was often seen late at night on an unfrequented road outside the city, carrying a plate of food, usually roast chicken, mashed potatoes and green peas, sometimes *congris* or gumbo. The food was left under a tree. This was called "paying off," and is practiced by Voodooiennes of today.

Nowadays all Voodoo practitioners in the United States use Marie Laveau's *gris-gris* following the teachings of the Widow Paris and her daughter. Strange-looking old women and witch doctors from New York, Chicago and the Pacific Coast came to New Orleans, some of them during the Laveau period, others many years afterward, to study and to carry home the art. In Houston and Harlem and Atlanta the same amulets and fetishes are used and the identical incantations are chanted. Chain order houses sell *gris-gris* invented by the Laveaus to every nook and corner of North America.

Marie II charged high prices for her services, though the amounts varied according to the wealth of her client. Everything was very businesslike. She had cards printed with her name and address and describing her work. These were distributed with amazing boldness, though she did not term herself a Voodooienne on the cards, but a "Healer."

She accepted no white client for less than ten dollars. This was sufficient to have one's fortune told and to purchase some simple good luck charm. Because of the notoriety she received practically everyone in the city must have visited her at least once. To go see Marie Laveau became one of the things a tourist in New Orleans must do, just as he was supposed to eat once in each of the famous restaurants and attend a performance at the French Opera House.

Her prices for regular and more serious clients sometimes ran to three or four figures. Businessmen might pay from $50 to $500 for her guidance in certain matters. At least one politician gave her $1,000 when he wanted to be elected a judge. He won the election. There were similar prices for winning the love of a desired man or woman, breaking up a marriage or bringing ruin to a rival either in a love affair or in business. The removal of an enemy by death cost from $500 to $1,000, at least that is what we are told.

There was a charge of ten dollars for powder to sprinkle on the front steps of an enemy's house (this was the most commonly used *gris-gris* of all) and the same charge for anti-*gris-gris* powder, which was supposed to counteract the first. It was not unusual for Marie to sell both powders to the two individuals concerned in the same Voodoo feud. More intricate charms were priced accordingly. If the undertaker's father bought that mummified baby for $20 he got a bargain. They are said to have cost at least $100 each.

"I never 'sociates wit' trashy peoples, white or colored," said Adele Brown, who despite her eighty years still peddles vegetables on the streets of New Orleans. "I has a good standin' wit' my friends and I is always careful. Sure, I remembers

that Marie Laveau. Man, you talk 'bout a hellcat—she was
the worst! I never has went wit' hoodoo people in my life,
but I seen some funny things. Marie Laveau owned half the
property 'round Rampart and St. Ann and you know how
she made it . . . I hates to think 'bout it.

"She used to give dances in lots of places and they was
dancin' for the devil. I don't mind the dancin' and I always
said there is a time to dance and a time to refrain from dancin',
but one time you got to refrain is when you is mixed up wit'
them hoodoo people. I see them people all 'round here now—
two-headed doctors and women what walks backward. Old
Marie Laveau looked just like the devil herself, and she's
settin' on a throne in Hell today. She used to walk 'round
this city like she owned every brick in the *banquette*, her.
She walked like a queen, wit' her head in the air and her eyes
on the stars and all that jewelry she'd bought wit' other
people's blood jinglin' and makin' a noise.

"She killed plenty people. Sure, she did. She could do anything and get by wit' it. She put curses on people to the fourth
generation, and you know that's a sin 'cause nobody but God
is supposed to do that. It says so in the Bible. She was always
breakin' up homes and families, and nobody could stop her.
She could call up spirits from the dead. She could make pictures fall off walls. I seen that happen lots of times.

"I used to spit three times and say my prayers every time
I seen her. I was a little child then and I didn't know much,
but I went to Sunday School and to church and I always has
had a feelin' for evil. My ma used to tell me to close my eyes
and not look at her, but sometimes I looked. I always been a
big Bible reader and a big prayer, and I knowed my Bible
and my prayin' was gonna protect me.

"One time when I was small some people want to take me
to her house. Me, I didn't want to go, but you know how
it is. I got to the gate and I hung back. I was half scared and

half curious. I said, 'I ain't goin' in that house. It's full of spirits and I don't want to see 'em,' and they say, 'Ah, come on, Adele!' and start hollerin' 'Adele's a scairty-cat' and stuff like that. They dragged me through that gate and the whole yard was full of banana trees and fig trees and the grass was up to my knees. I'd done heared 'bout a snake she kept and I didn't want to go in no further, but they kept pullin' me.

"When I got inside the front door I started shiverin' and shakin' all over. I seen a skeleton of a little child clingin' to the outside of her *armoire*, and her settin' on the floor, rockin' forward and backward and laughin' and laughin'. Me, I was so scared I run out of that house screamin' at the top of my voice. From that day on I never messed wit' hoodoo people. Sometimes I wakes up in the middle of the night right now and I still sees the skeleton of that poor little child hangin' on the outside of her *armoire*, and her settin' there, rockin' back and forth and laughin' and laughin'."

# 12
# C'est l'Amour, Maman!

AGING Creoles in New Orleans have a favorite Marie Laveau love story. There was, they will tell you, once a certain Monsieur S., a very wealthy old bachelor, who owned a handsome mansion not far from the Laveau cottage.

Monsieur S. fell madly in love with the lovely daughter of another Creole gentleman and, despite the fact that he was old enough to be her grandfather, came to court the young lady. The girl would have none of him, but her father, whose finances were in a somewhat dismal state, approved the match and attempted to force his daughter to marry the man. When she flatly refused the father locked the girl in a cabin near the lake, and here each night Monsieur S., always attended by the father, came to woo her. It is said that the father would use harsh words and threats, on one occasion even beating the girl severely in the presence of her decrepit suitor. Nightly her piteous sobbing could be heard by passersby.

And it was all in vain. The girl swore she would die rather than marry Monsieur S. He was ugly and repulsive and, besides, she had already given her heart to a young soldier and adventurer, whom she expected to return any day now from the West Indies, where he had gone to make his fortune.

At last, in desperation, the father and the rich man went together to seek the services of Marie Laveau. The sorceress listened to their story and informed them that she could promise that the marriage would take place. Powders were given the father to be placed in the girl's food, and Monsieur S. was given a *gris-gris* consisting of the dried testicles of a black cat, which he was to wear close to his own genitals to relieve his condition of impotency. She advised the men to be patient and not to ask the girl to marry Monsieur for a period of two weeks.

One night two weeks later the girl, very pale, her voice trembling, announced to her father that she had changed her mind and that she was ready to marry the old man. Monsieur S. fell to his knees and kissed her hands and the father nearly fainted with joy.

Plans were made immediately to have the wedding take place at once. In another fortnight all of Creole society packed the Cathedral for the ceremony. There was much whispering and clucking of tongues as the lovely bride, wearing an exquisite satin gown and a string of magnificent pearls—a wedding gift from her husband—stood beside the aged man with the slightly bent knees and the coal-black toupee while the priest united them in a state of matrimony. That evening there was an elaborate reception in the mansion of Monsieur S., where champagne flowed as from a fountain and there was every sort of delicious and rare food.

As the guests imbibed freely of the champagne, the party grew gayer and there were demands that the bride and groom dance alone on the ballroom floor. At last, his wrinkled face flushed with excitement, Monsieur led his slender bride to the center of the floor, signaled the musicians, and, as they began a brisk waltz, swung the new Madame S. across the room in his arms. For a few moments he seemed half his years.

But, very suddenly, he stopped dancing and the guests saw the bride break away from his grasp and step back with one hand across her mouth. As Monsieur S., his face turning from red to purple, swayed for a few seconds and then crumpled to the floor, she uttered a shriek that caused the music to stop with a crash and brought the spectators to her side. A doctor was summoned, but it was too late. Monsieur S. was dead. The excitement and the exercise had been too much for his heart.

They still talk about it. Madame S. inherited a large fortune and was able to summon her young lover home from the Indies. After a year, during which she, being properly reared, observed conventional mourning, they were married and lived happily ever afterward. And it is said that when people asked Marie Laveau a question regarding the affair, she would look at them with some amusement in her strange eyes and would say, with the trace of a smile, "I promised only that the wedding would take place."

Love probably brought more people to the Laveau cottage than anything else. New Orleans is a very romantic city and the Creoles were an amorous race. Men were always asking Marie to help them to win certain girls, and the girls came to her seeking husbands.

The most commonly used *gris-gris* in affairs of the affections always included something belonging to the object of adoration. A young girl would be told to bring Marie the glove of the man she loved. This would be filled with a mixture of steel dust, sugar and honey—the sugar and honey were to "sweeten" the man, the steel dust was for *power*—and the girl was instructed to sleep with the glove under her mattress. One keeps wondering about ants!

If a woman wanted a married man, Marie would write the name of the man and his wife on a piece of paper, place the paper in a bladder (obtained from the slaughterhouse), and hang it in the sun to dry. The man would leave his wife, and all the woman had to do then, to keep him, was to use sufficient *gris-gris* of such types as love powders and oils. She might be even more successful if during their "love play" she would measure his sexual organ with a piece of string and tie nine knots in this string and wear it about her person from that day on. As long as she wore this he would be "tied to her."

Another way a woman could hold a man was to take some of the blood from her menstrual flow and mix it in her man's food. Once the man ate this he was hers forever and she had him completely under her domination. Negroes in New Orleans today swear that this is still practiced, and Negro men live in fear of it being done to them. Every henpecked husband in the lower colored strata is the subject of such speculation. Negresses will sometimes boast of having done this to their men; they refer to this as a "Marie Laveau trick."

Parents would often ask Marie to prevent their daughter or son from marrying a person of whom they did not approve. One of her favorite *gris-gris* to break up such an affair was a mixture of gunpowder, mud from a wasp nest, flaxseed, cayenne pepper, BB shots, filé, bluestone and dragon's blood. All these were mixed and then thrown on the front steps of the undesirable person's house.

Sometimes when business was not as brisk as she liked it Marie II would create her own. One such instance is a favorite story among those who remember her. On this occasion a young man came to her house, complaining that he was "broke" and hungry. Marie, somewhat in need of cash herself, determined to make some money for both of them. She stretched the man out upon a couch in the front room of her cottage, covered him with a sheet and lighted candles at his head and feet. Then she went outside and sat on her front steps. As neighbors passed, she burst into sobs and loud cries of grief. There was the corpse of a dear friend within, she told them, and there was no money with which to defray his burial expenses. She knew the Negro's love for funerals and "wakes," and soon the room in which the "corpse" lay was crowded with the curious. Marie then took a stand by the couch, a bowl in her hand and as the visitors passed they dropped in coins. Soon the bowl was filled, so she requested that she be left alone with her dead. The room emptied, the "corpse" sat up, and he and Marie divided the money.

She did the same sort of thing with the lovers who came to her. She would attempt to create upheavals on all sides and to profit from every angle.

"That kind of foolin' was always wit' white people," said Mary Ellis. "She was never interested in colored folks for those things, 'cause she knowed they didn't have enough money to make it worth her while. White people was different. She knew their ways; she had learned men's ways from the women and the women's ways from the men. Sometimes she'd really *fix* 'em. She'd git a gal for some married man and when he and this gal got to layin' up, Marie Laveau would see that his wife found out about it. She wouldn't tell the wife herself, understand? She would just start it spreadin' by word of mouth 'til the wife got hold of it. Then the wife would come to her to git her husband back. That would cost her money. After that the man would be told his wife had found out he was messin' 'round and he'd better stop it. In cases like that all she had to do was fool the white people— and that was easy. Sometimes she'd collect both ways, and she'd git money from both the wife and the husband. God, that was a smart woman!"

Mary said that most of the things she knew about Marie Laveau had been told her by an aunt who had been a Voodoo.

"My aunt told me one time she had trouble wit' her landlord. He told her to git out of her house or he'd have her put in jail," Mary said. "He even sent a policeman after her. The next day she went to Marie Laveau and she told my aunt to burn twelve blue candles in a barrel half full of sand. She done that and my aunt never did have to move and she never went to jail in her whole life. Marie Laveau used to tell people not to burn candles in church 'cause that gived their luck to somebody else, so they burned 'em in her house instead. She'd tell my aunt, 'If you gonna fool 'em, fool 'em good, Alice.' She was real good to my aunt. She even taught her a Voodoo song. It went like this:

> St. Peter, St. Peter, open the door,
> I'm callin' you, come to me!
> St. Peter, St. Peter, open the door . . .

"That's all I can remember. Marie Laveau used to call St. Peter somethin' like 'Laba.' She called St. Michael 'Daniel Blanc,' and St. Anthony 'Yon Sue.' There was another one she called 'On Za Tier'; I think that was St. Paul. I never did know where them names come from. They sounded Chinee to me. You know the Chinee emperor sent her a shawl? She wore it all the time, my aunt told me."

The shawl from the Emperor of China was another example of the Laveau boasting. Probably it had been given to one of the Maries by a seafaring customer. The Widow Paris bragged of having been kissed by Lafayette when he visited New Orleans. Once another member of the household gave a visitor a vase which, it was claimed, had been presented to the Widow Paris by Louis Philippe.

"*C'est l'amour, oui maman, c'est l'amour!*" chanted the cultists as dawn brought their ceremonies to an end. Yet we have little definite knowledge of the private amours of Marie II.

We must remember that Marie II was understudying her mother, that she was a sort of living legend and that professionally she was an extension of another person. We do know that she never married.

"Marie Laveau was an old maid," said Mrs. Dixon, an old white woman who claimed to remember her well. "She had plenty men, but she never married none of them. I guess she was too smart. She knew a lot about love, though.

"My mother had a friend named Mrs. Flaguet. Her husband used to beat her all the time. He'd kick her out of bed and make her sleep on the floor. He'd come home drunk and bring fancy women with big hats into her home.

"Well, she got tired of it, so she went to see Marie Laveau. That great Voodoo woman was sitting in the front room of her house with her eyes closed and hardly any lights in the room, but she said right away, 'Come on in, Mrs. Flaguet, I've been waiting for you.' In Creole, you know; she didn't speak much English, of course, and neither did my mother's friend—we're all very French. Well, Mrs. Flaguet was certainly surprised. She said, 'How did you know my name?' And Marie Laveau said, 'I know everything, Mrs. Flaguet. I know your husband beats you and makes you sleep on the floor, and that ain't right.'

"Mrs. Flaguet broke down then and started crying. I remember my mother said she cried so much she ruined her veil. Then she told Marie Laveau all about her trouble. And you know what Marie Laveau told her to do? It isn't very nice, but I'll tell you. She said for her to take a towel she and her husband used when they was together and to wave it in his face when he was sleeping. She said it was sure to work.

"Do you know that after Mrs. Flaguet did that her husband ain't never hit her again? And he never did put her out of the bed again or fool with other women. They lived together for thirty-eight years and they died the same week, her first and him right afterward. You see she had such a hold on him he couldn't even live without her. He had been *fixed* by Marie Laveau.

"She could do all those things. You know she invented Follow-Me Water; if a lady puts some of this on her handkerchief and waves the handkerchief in the face of a young man she likes he is sure to follow her. She used to sell men Go-Away Powder. They'd throw this on a woman they wanted to get rid of and she would go away. Another thing she'd tell men to do to stop women from bothering them was to make crosses with brown chalk on their front steps. If any woman stepped on one of those brown crosses she'd fall down and break one of her legs. She knew all that kind of thing. That's why she never got married. She didn't need to have any man bossing her around the place."

Jennie Collins, a very black old woman, said, with a giggle, "That Marie Laveau sure had the men following her. Me, I always thought my pa was messin' wit' her, but I didn't never tell my ma that. Did you know she had children all over the place? Some was almost white and some was almost black. Nobody never did know who they fathers was. Her and her brother John. Did you ever hear 'bout John Laveau? That was a rascal. He was what the womens called a sweet. He never did no work in his life and Marie Laveau helped him git women wit' love powders and all that stuff. He was sure a sweet, all right."

Jennie probably exaggerated about the number of children, but undoubtedly Marie II did have many lovers, both white and colored. At least several of them were prominent men of the city, one being a rather distinguished judge.

Her relationship with Lafcadio Hearn was public gossip around 1880. Hearn himself wrote of having lived in the house of a woman whom he describes, somewhat curiously, as "a vampire." As disliked personally as his genius was admired, Hearn seems to have spent nearly all his sojourn in New Orleans in the company of Negroes and Voodoos. He was an undersized and repulsive little man. A modern psychologist could have explained what a terrible burden of complexes and frustrations must have made him shut himself

off from his own kind and race and seek association with another sort, but then he was dismissed as being guilty of depravity. A year after his death the New York *Sun* published an
account of how a Negress in Cincinnati was claiming to be
his widow and was fighting for a share of the American
royalties on his fine literary works, and told how he had
married a Japanese girl and had spent his last years in Japan.
The New Orleans *Daily News*, reprinting the story on
August 6, 1906, recalled how he had spent his years in New
Orleans "with Negroes—not the ordinary cornfield type, but
the Congo priestesses and prophetesses; as a matter of fact
with no less a personage than Marie Laveau, the Voodoo
queen." It is interesting to wonder what a child of this pair
would have been like. Unfortunately Marie II was in her
fifties when she met Hearn.

He was a late lover. All her life she had been pursued by
men. Most of her suitors, we are told, were coolly rejected.
Many a gallant, seeking her services, became intrigued with
the exotic quadroon, but he had small chance of success.
Apparently she preferred to choose her own sweethearts,
rather than to be won by masculine persuasions. Even in her
love affairs she was boss; and most of her lovers, in keeping
with the mystery surrounding her, remain anonymous.

Jennie Collins said, "She knew all other people's business,
but they didn't know much about her. She kept things like her
mens quiet. But, don't worry, she had 'em. She knew all about
love and stuff like that.

"She would tell young gals what wanted husbands to take
the juice from four lemons and rub the legs of their beds
wit' it for nine nights. Every night they got to put a glass
of water under the bed. When they git in bed they had to
lie still wit' their knees bent up and spread wide, and they
was supposed to wish hard as they could until they fell asleep.
That is one thing I believes in, 'cause I has seen it work.

"Another thing she used to always tell gals to do was to take a dime and a piece of stale bread and git on the ferry goin' 'cross the river. When they gits in the middle they is supposed to throw the money and bread in the water. Then they goes to church and makes a Flyin' Novena. That is still good. I knows gals what does it now."

# 13
# Doctor Jim

THE most important man in the life of Marie II was never her lover. He was Jim Alexander, who called himself "Doctor Jim," in the tradition of all Voodoo witch doctors, and with his arrival in New Orleans Marie faced the first real challenge to her omnipotence.

Doctor Jim was three-quarters Indian, one-quarter Negro, and he liked to pass as a Mexican. He had been practicing in the State of Mississippi for years before moving into the territory dominated by Marie Laveau, and when he came he brought with him much experience in the field, a reputation as a successful healer, and a white wife, who was a fairly well known Voodooienne herself. His powers of healing are said to have been remarkable. According to some persons who remember him, "He was cleverer than Marie Laveau at makin' you well when you was sick."

There are no accounts of his activities until the late 1870's, but after that he was a familiar figure in New Orleans. He is said to have made a great deal of money and was more successful at retaining it than Marie. "The truth is that all the Laveaus was heavy gamblers," said Nathan Hobley, a Negro of great age, who now describes himself as a "divine healer." "Doctor Jim bought land. He owned all the property between Gentilly and Spanish Fort."

Old Nathan probably knows more about Jim Alexander than anyone living. He claims that most of the knowledge he now applies in his own practices was learned from that witch doctor at first hand.

"He was tall and straight and looked like an Indian," Nathan said. "Lots of people called him 'Indian Jim.' He was the only person had enough nerve to buck up against Marie Laveau. She got mad when some of her people started going to Indian Jim instead of her, and first thing she done was to get the law to go and raid his house. When that didn't do no good she put *gris-gris* on him—the worst kind she had. But it just didn't work. I guess his *gris-gris* was as strong as hers. Sometimes they'd meet in the street and they'd call each other names and fight. Once it got so bad some people called the police, but Marie Laveau got rid of them. She wanted to fight this out her own way. After that he began to go to some of her meetings and they sort of patched it up. But from then on it was Marie Laveau that lost some of her business. People went to him and she couldn't stop them, so they kind of worked together. She knew more than he did about most kinds of hoodoo and she began teaching him some of her tricks. He never did much besides healing, though. He was better at that than she was.

"You know his real name was Laurinsky Avery. That didn't come out until a long time, when he got into trouble once. He outlived Marie Laveau and he did a big business after she was gone. I remember his wife good. She was the only white Voodoo woman around then so far as I know. She was sure crazy about him and jealous because he had something that got the women. I don't think there was ever nothing like that between him and Marie Laveau. You see she was lots older than he was—and then she had other men at that time."

The *Daily Picayune* ran a story of the Laveau-Alexander feud during the first years of its existence, titling it:

TROUBLE AMONG THE VOUDOUS

The contest is occasioned by a disputed point of faith between Marie Laveau and Dr. Jim, the great physician, who is supposed by his disciples to hold in his hands the issues of life and death. The consequences of this antagonism between the priest and the high priestess is [sic] an unusual shortage of beef hearts and black crepe. Their violent discussions a few nights since demanded the interposition of the police, and a number of them were arrested, nevertheless, it had no effect in allaying the fever of excitement, and the conflict is still waged with vehement antipathy.

Yet some years later the antipathy seems to have been put aside by both Marie and Indian Jim. "I came to New Orleans in 1880," one old colored man said, "and Jim Alexander was always with Marie Laveau then. She was sure smart, but he was just as smart in some ways." He added, "Those troubled in spirit went to Marie Laveau, but they went to Doctor Jim when they was hurtin'."

Nathan Hobley said, "He used to give me money all the time to go with him to cure people. He sure did well. He bought a house on Orleans near Johnson Street. I can see it now. It had a long gallery down the side and the last two rooms was his church. He received his visitors there and him and his wife lived in the other rooms."

Nathan could also remember Papa Sol. "He used to help Indian Jim," he explained. "He was pretty good and sometimes he used to make Marie Laveau mad as a hornet, but he wasn't no good after Jim Alexander died. Couldn't do nothing on his own.

"I remember one time me and Alexander broke up evil spirits across the river in Algiers," said Nathan. "There was a girl over there about twelve years old who was possessed with a devil. One night she was going from room to room with a lamp in her hand, when all of a sudden she began whirling like a broke watch spring. Finally she landed on top a table, but a minute later she was whirling again.

"The next day she was in the kitchen and every piece of wood jumped out of the basket by the stove and smashed right through a shut window and went flying out into the yard. This was in 1882, and Algiers and New Orleans was both excited about it. Her father moved her to another house about nine blocks off. That night the piano began to play. It not only played, but it moved itself around the room without nobody touching it.

"They sent for Alexander and he asked me to go with him. When we got to the house he lit three candles and filled a tin bucket with beer. He sent everybody out of the room and then he sprinkled the beer all over the furniture and the floor, in the four corners of the room; he even threw some up at the ceiling. We went over to the first house where the girl had done the whirling and did the same thing. There has never been any evil spirits in Algiers since.

"Doctor Jim always used beer for that kind of treatment. One night spirits was throwing pillows out a window on Claiborne Street and he and me went with the beer and stopped that. You see the evil spirits drank the beer and was satisfied and went away. Both New Orleans and Algiers was full of evil spirits at that time, but we sure did clean 'em out. You don't never hear about things like that now, you know. This place owes a lot to Jim Alexander.

"Of course he held other kinds of services, too. He was one of the best hoodoo dancers I ever saw in my life. He would dance naked with hot coals on his head and the women would go wild. He was wonderful!"

He does seem to have been rather wonderful, but he was not smart enough to keep out of what Negroes sometimes refer to as "police trouble." On several occasions Jim Alexander went to jail, and his dances were constantly being interrupted by the law. He lacked Marie Laveau's skill in handling the police, and his so-called dances had a sex angle that the law didn't like.

The dance for which he became famous was not quite as Nathan Hobley described it, but it was sufficiently fantastic to attract much attention. It was a bizarre combination of the

Calinda and an Indian war dance, performed in tights and with a candle balanced on his head. The *Times Democrat*, describing a raid by the police in May, 1889, told of discovering ten Negro men lying on the floor, all of them nearly nude, and fifteen white women sitting in chairs placed in a circle about them. In the center, Jim Alexander was executing his dance, wearing "a pair of drawers with a large mesh and a blue sash." Two of the girls present were only seventeen years of age. Also among the attendants was Lou Jackson, a white prostitute, known both for her interest in Voodoo and for an attachment to Doctor Jim.

Alexander also gave dances on barges out on Lake Pontchartrain. He was a good showman. In the yard of his home in Orleans Street was a pool in which he kept two alligators. Witnesses vowed that when he called them by name the alligators rose out of the water and came to him. This was the sort of thing that increased his prestige greatly in the Voodoo world. It was almost as good as the snakes that were supposed to inhabit the Laveau residence.

Doctor Jim came to a sudden and violent end. One Yoy Livaudais, a simple-minded boy in his neighborhood, hit him in the head with a rock. An abscess formed and he died shortly afterward.

It was many years before his estate was settled, and then his supposed wealth was found to have been very much exaggerated. All the witch doctor left his wife was his home and $3,006.50. It was also revealed that his name was neither James Alexander nor Laurinsky Avery, but Charles LaFontaine. Perhaps, as the newspapers suggested, his wife, Clemence, had hoarded some cash, but of owning "all the property between Gentilly and Spanish Fort" there was no trace. What became of the money he made—and it was substantiated that he had made a great deal—remains a mystery.

# 14
# Marie the Sainted

ON June 16, 1881, the newspapers of New Orleans announced that Marie Laveau was dead. This was the Widow Paris.

Immediately the most fantastic legends were born. At the moment of her passing the earth beneath the cottage had trembled and lightning and thunder had passed through the room. There had been the sounds of creaking chains and turning wheels, and shrieks of joy from the fiends of Hell. In reality old Marie died peacefully, in her sleep.

The most astonishing fact about her death was that she had departed this life in an atmosphere as impressively Catholic as if she had been the Mother Superior of a convent. In her last years she had accomplished a startling, though characteristic enough, metamorphosis. She had renounced the Zombi and all his works, denied any connection with the Voodoos and returned to the Church. Thereafter some members of the family expressed passionate indignation at even an implication that she had ever been a Voodooienne.

Most of the morning newspapers the morning after her death carried stories of her saintliness. One of these, which appeared in the *Daily Picayune*, was so naïve that either its author was not a native of the city or he was very young and knew nothing of Voodoo. It is probably one of the most interesting documents in existence regarding the Marie Laveaus, stating:

DEATH OF MARIE LAVEAU, A WOMAN WITH A WONDERFUL HISTORY,
ALMOST A CENTURY OLD—CARRIED TO THE
TOMB YESTERDAY EVENING

Those who have passed by the quaint old house on St. Ann, between Rampart and Burgundy streets, with the high frail-looking fence in front over which a tree or two is visible, have been within the last few years pleased to notice through the open gateway a decrepid [sic] old lady with snow-white hair, and a smile of peace and contentment lighting up her golden features. For a few years past she has been missed from her accustomed place. The feeble old lady lay upon her bed with her daughter and grandchildren around her, ministering to her wants.

On Wednesday the invalid sank into the sleep which knows no waking. Those whom she had befriended crowded into the little room where she was exposed, in order to take a last look at the features, smiling even in death, of her who had been so kind to them.

At 5 o'clock yesterday evening Marie Laveau was buried in her family tomb in St. Louis Cemetery. Her remains were followed to the grave by a large concourse of people, the most prominent and the most humble joining in paying their last respects to the dead. Father Mignot conducted the funeral services.

Marie Laveau was born ninety-eight years ago. Her father was a rich planter, who was prominent in all public affairs, and served in the Legislature of this State. Her mother was Marguerite Henry, and her grandmother was Marguerite Semard. All were beautiful women of color. The gift of beauty was hereditary in the family, and Marie inherited it in the fullest degree. When she was twenty-five years old she was led to the altar by Jacques Paris, a carpenter. This marriage took place at the St. Louis Cathedral, Père Antoine, of beloved memory, conducting the service, and Mr. Mazureau, the famous lawyer, acting as witness. A year afterward Mr. Paris disappeared, and no one knows to this day what became of him. After waiting a year for his return she married Capt. Christophe Glapion. The latter was also very prominent here, and served with distinction in the battalion of men of Santo Domingo, under D'Aquin, with Jackson in the war of 1815. . . .

Besides being very beautiful Marie was also very wise. She was skillful in the practice of medicine and was acquainted with the valuable healing qualities of indigenous herbs.

She was very successful as a nurse, wonderful stories being

told of her exploits at the sickbed. In yellow fever and cholera epidemics she was always called upon to nurse the sick, and always responded promptly. Her skill and knowledge earned her the friendship and approbation of those sufficiently cultivated, but the ignorant attributed her success to unnatural means and held her in constant dread.

Notably in 1853 a committee of gentlemen, appointed at a mass meeting held at Globe Hall, waited on Marie and requested her on behalf of the people to minister to the fever-stricken. She went out and fought the pestilence where it was thickest and many alive today owe their salvation to her devotion. . . . Marie was also very pious and took delight in strengthening the allegiance of souls to the church. She would sit with the condemned in their last moments and endeavor to turn their last thoughts to Jesus. Whenever a prisoner excited her pity Marie would labor incessantly to obtain his pardon, or at least a commutation of sentence, and she generally succeeded.

A few years ago, before she lost control of her memory, she was rich in interesting reminiscences of the early history of this city. She spoke often of the young American Governor Claiborne, and told how his child-wife he brought with him from Tennessee [and who] died of the yellow fever shortly after his arrival, with the dead babe upon her bosom, was buried in a corner of the old American Cemetery. She spoke sometimes of the strange little man with the wonderful bright eyes, Aaron Burr, who was so polite and so dangerous. She loved to talk of Lafayette, who visited New Orleans over half a century ago. The great Frenchman came to see her at her house, and kissed her on the forehead at parting.

She remembered the old French General, Humbert, and was one of the few colored people who escorted to the tomb long since dismantled in the Catholic Cemetery the withered and grizzly remains of the hero of Castlebar. Probably she knew Father Antoine better than any living in those days—for he the priest and she the nurse met at the dying bedside of hundreds of people—she to close the faded eyes in death, and he to waft the soul over the river to the realms of eternal joy.

All in all Marie Laveau was a most wonderful woman. Doing good for the sake of doing good alone, she obtained no reward, ofttimes meeting with prejudices and loathing; she was nevertheless contented and did not lag in her work. She always had the cause of the people at heart and was with them in all things. During the late rebellion she proved her loyalty to the South at every opportunity and fully dispensed help to those who suffered in defense of the "lost cause."

Her last days were spent surrounded by sacred pictures and other evidences of religion, and she died with a firm trust in Heaven. While God's sunshine plays around the little tomb where her remains are buried, by the side of her second husband, and her sons and daughters, Marie Laveau's name will not be forgotten in New Orleans.

This was written of the Marie Laveau who had danced with snakes, who had drunk the warm blood of the sacrifice, who had chanted Congo songs to the tempo of the tom-toms, who had crept through the streets in the dead of the night to leave coffins and conjure balls on the doorsteps of her enemies. This was written of the Marie Laveau who had been accused of committing human sacrifice.

And it was not the only such article. Almost all the papers carried similar ones. But there was one dissenter. The next day, June 18, a writer published in the *New Orleans Democrat* the following denunciation of the hymns of praise. He was so angry he did not even bother to use the correct spelling of the Laveau name. Such misspellings were commonplace.

### A SAINTED WOMAN

Who has been stuffing our contemporaries in the matter of the defunct Voudou queen, Marie Lavoux? For they have undoubtedly been stuffed, nay crammed, by some huge practical joker. The informant for all is evidently the same, as the stories of the *Picayune, Item,* and *States* consist admirably in their uniform departure from historical fact. According to these esteemed but deluded contemporaries, Marie Lavoux was a saint, who had spent a life of self-sacrifice and abnegation in doing good to her fellow mortals, and whose immaculate spirit was all but too pure for this world.

One of them even went so far in his enthusiasm as to publish

a touching interview with the sainted woman, in which the reporter boasts of having deposited a chaste kiss on her holy forehead. We are sorry for that reporter if his story is true, for,
if he really believes it all, his only consolation is in the fact that
greenness is the color of hope. These fictions had one good
result, for they created a vast amount of merriment among the
old Creole residents, and in fact among all men of mature age
who knew the social history of their time in New Orleans.

The fact is that the least said about Marie Lavoux's sainted
life, etc., the better. She was, up to an advanced age, the prime
mover and soul of the indecent orgies of the ignoble Voudous;
and to her influence may be attributed the fall of many a vir-
tuous woman. It is true that she had redeeming traits. It is a
peculiar quality of the old race of Creole Negroes that they are
invariably kind-hearted and charitable. Marie Lavoux made no
exception. But talk about her morality and kiss her sainted brow
—pouah!!!

Thus it was, saint or witch, Marie Laveau received even
at her death the publicity she seemed so to love during her
reign over the Voodoos. Even her age was exaggerated. The
certificate of death stated that she was ninety-eight. Board of
Health records in New Orleans do show the birth of a Marie
Laveau in 1783, but if that is the Voodoo queen, then she was
about thirty-six when she married Paris and forty when she
bore Glapion the first of their fifteen children. That does not
make sense. The name was a common one. There were many
Marie Laveaus born during the last two decades of the eight-
eenth century. There were even several women of that name
who lived in the same block of St. Ann Street during the
time she lived there. Some may have been relatives, others
probably were not. To add to the confusion there were Marie
Labeauds and Marie Lavauds. The physician present at her
final illness, Doctor J. B. Bass of New York, later made a
public statement in which he said that then he did not believe
her to be as old as the family had claimed. He judged her
as being somewhere in her late eighties.

Nowhere in the accounts of the death or the funeral is there a word about Marie II. Legally, strange as it may seem, Marie II died with her mother.

There is, however, mention of a single daughter, Madame Legendre, who is described as being "majestic in appearance" and "nearly white." She was the widow of a white man and the mother of several nearly white children. What had become of Marie II and of John Laveau? Had all the other children of old Marie died or gone away?

There are several theories. One is that Madame Legendre was so anxious for the family to attain a respectable reputation that she somehow secured dominance over Marie II and banished her from the St. Ann Street cottage after their mother's death. Another is that Madame Legendre and Marie II were the same person. The latter is not impossible, but it is not very probable. Madame Legendre bore the reputation of being a highly religious woman, who though she sometimes told fortunes and invited people to burn candles and tapers before the altar in the house, despised anything that was tainted with Voodooism. It was probably she who had convinced the newspaper reporters of her mother's saintliness.

It was Madame Legendre who spent the next few years in a fervent effort to purify the family tree. When George W. Cable wrote of Marie Laveau as one of the greatest sorceresses of all time, Madame uttered protestations, threatened libel suits, wept, swore and made novenas. If this was Marie II putting on an act it seems without purpose. No, we can be sure that Marie II must have been a separate being and certainly a source of much displeasure to Madame.

A reporter for the *Daily Picayune* (he sounds like the same one who penned the sentimental account at the time of the death of the Widow Paris) called at the Laveau cottage and read its occupants a part of Cable's impressions of Marie Laveau and a few days later published a story of his visit—

this was five years after the passing of old Marie—and of Madame's reaction, telling how:

Although it was an April day, there was a fire in Marie Laveau's old room. Around it sat Mme. Legendre and three of her daughters, one of them a chubby child across her lap. There are still three generations in the place.

Every one of the group was comely. Madame, although her heavy mass of hair is turning as white as that of her mother, still shows the sign of beauty which she inherited. Tall, majestic, graceful, the eye still flashing fire, and with firm step . . . she rules her household, even if she has not the tact of Marie Laveau to extend her realm and number her subjects by the hundreds. This is what the reporter read to the group, in the little room of the old house, beside the fire that failed to brighten the walls, but cast a glow upon the faces. It is from "Creole Slave Songs," in the April *Century*, by George W. Cable:

". . . I once saw, in her extreme old age, the famed Marie Laveau. Her dwelling was in a quadroon quarter of New Orleans, but a step or two from Congo Square, a small adobe cabin just off the sidewalk, scarcely higher than its close board fence, whose batten gate yielded to the touch and revealed the crazy doors and windows spread wide to the warm air, and one or two tawny faces within, whose expression was divided between a pretense of contemptuous inattention and a frowning resentment of the intrusion. In the center of a small room whose ancient cypress floor was worn with scrubbing and sprinkled with crumbs of soft brick—a Creole affectation of superior cleanliness—sat quaking with feebleness in an ill-looking old rocking chair, her body bowed, and her wild, gray witch's tresses hanging about her shriveled yellow neck, the queen of the Voudous . . . her daughter was also present, a woman of some seventy years, and a most striking and majestic figure. In feature, stature and bearing she was regal. One had but to look on her, impute her brilliance—too untamable and severe to be called charms or graces—to her mother, and remember what New Orleans was long years ago, to understand how the name of Marie Laveau should have driven itself inextricably into the traditions of the town and times. . . ."

None of the four women waited until the reading was over.

Several times the reporter was interrupted by angry laughs of derision and angry cries of "It's a lie. It's a lie." When the reading was over they were quite beside themselves with rage. Madame was walking up and down the room with quick sharp steps, making vain attempts to express herself in English and then relapsing into scorching French. . . .

It went on and on. Madame Legendre threatened to have the house torn down as soon as she had sufficient money to build a new one. She was tired of it all. Too many curious persons were bothering her and the children. Artists came and wanted to paint pictures. Newspapermen and writers would no longer be welcome. They had been received kindly, then had gone off to write untruths. The house would be boarded up and the front gate locked.

Somewhere in or near the city Marie II must have been worried about her future.

# 15
# Knock on My Tombstone

MARIE GLAPION was only fifty-four when the Widow Paris died. She was at the height of her career. During the years that followed she remained "Marie Laveau" to the majority of the Voodoos and to the uneducated class of Negroes, who did not read the newspapers. She managed, therefore, to retain her position as supreme ruler over the queens and witch doctors of the period and it is known that she appeared at some of the St. John's Eve meetings in the 1880's. She also still possessed the Maison Blanche.

But with her mother's death she had lost a great deal, for the most lucrative part of her business had been done in the St. Ann Street cottage. This must have been a bitter blow both to her pride and to her purse, and she must have fought against her exile with all her strength. However, to the readers of the papers Marie Laveau was dead. No doubt many of them knew it could not be the Marie Laveau they knew, but if they called at the house it was to have the door shut in their faces by Madame Legendre.

"Marie Glapion was an outcast from her family," said Virgie Wilson, an old colored woman. "You see, that Madame Legendre, her sister, was so stuck up that she done denied her. She run John Laveau out of the house, too, and didn't have nobody there but her and her two daughters. They wanted to pass for white. The daughters both married white men and their children is passing right here in New Orleans now. 'Course they done changed their names a couple of times and has forgot they was ever Laveaus or even that they come from Madame Legendre."

Marie II lived in the Maison Blanche for some years and most of her livelihood was earned by acting as a procuress for white men who wanted to meet quadroon and mulatto girls. Later she seems to have left the lakefront and returned to the city.

"She was livin' on Bourbon Street around 1888," recalled Edna Martin, who said she had been her neighbor during that period. "She told fortunes and messed wit' a lot of hoodoo stuff, but she was losin' her trade."

This was denied by Gertrude Apple, who said she, too, was a neighbor around that time. "She was the biggest hoodoo woman in town in 1890," Gertrude said.

A rather strange statement came from Alex Pique, a former postman. "I delivered a stack of mail addressed to Marie Laveau to that St. Ann Street house as late as 1887," he said. "Almost all of it was registered. I don't know exactly who was living there then." Was Madame Legendre handling the Marie Laveau correspondence? There probably had always been customers who wrote from out of town, seeking services of various sorts.

But, on the whole, the memories of Marie II began to fade somewhere in the late 1880's, and she seems to dissolve slowly into a state of non-existence, as if she had been a ghost or a mirage. There is no sudden end.

No one, for instance, can agree about how or when she died. The simplest deduction regarding the whole affair is that she lost herself completely in the Negro world. She may not have been any less important to the Voodoos when the end came, but except for them she was obscure and almost forgotten. Her prestige was to return after the coming of death.

There are many persons who insist that Marie II was drowned in Lake Pontchartrain during the late 1890's. Old colored women will often tell you stories about this.

"Marie Laveau was in her house out by the lake when the storm come up," said Louise Butler. "She was givin' a big Voodoo dance. The storm swept the house away and her and all them hoodoos with her. God punished them wicked people with flood." Louise thought this took place in 1899, but added, "I ain't got no head for dates and it could have been a year or so before or after that."

"It was in 1884," said Myrtle Rose White. "She was sleepin' in her bed and the house was washed away wit' her in it. That was the end of Marie Laveau and there was weepin' and grievin' from one end of this country to the other." Myrtle Rose was a Marie Laveau enthusiast. "She was the best woman ever lived," she said. "You know she died poor 'cause she had given all her money away."

"They was having them a time out there one St. John's Eve," said Catherine Woods. "Marie Laveau called for everybody to run out into the lake like they always done. She led 'em and she stepped down in a hole and never come up. People always said she was gone to see Papa La Bas."

But as often as not she survives the storm.

"She got washed away in a big storm, but she never died," swore Alice Reno. "She floated five days on a log and was swept in to shore. She never even suffered from exposure. She was too *powerful* to let nothin' hurt her. She lived for years after that."

It is not always Lake Pontchartrain. Sometimes it is Bayou St. John. There was a Voodoo belief that if one walked into the Bayou St. John on St. John's Eve any spell would be washed away, but the immersion must be complete, until the water covered the individual's head. There was a certain place at which this was done, and it was known as the Cure Spot. It is very likely this was the same as the Wishing Spot.

Doris Gibson claims this is where Marie II was almost drowned. "She walked into the water and disappeared complete," said Doris. "Everybody went home and thought she was dead. Five days later they found her floatin' around, clingin' to a log. She was sick, but she got well."

"When the storm come up," said Rose Keaton, "she was in the Cure Spot. A week after that they found her sittin' in a tree that was floatin' on the Bayou. She was singin' her hoodoo songs and wasn't hurt at all."

But Sophie Key contended "that peoples gits all mixed up. Some says she was in her house and the house got washed away. They got it wrong. You see, Marie Laveau could walk on the water and that's what she was doin' when the storm come. She was walkin' 'round on the lake singin' and prayin' and the water 'neath her feets got unsteady and the waves was rockin' and all. All of a sudden a big wave come up and she fell down and broke the water and started sinkin'. But a tree come by and she caught on to that. She was floatin' on that tree almost a week before they found her."

"She was dead when they found her," said Annabelle Kate Tricou. "Her body floated in to shore and her eyes was closed and her hands folded jest like she was already laid out at her wake. There was cryin' and weepin' all over New Orleans. The people knowed a great woman had passed from their midst."

But it was Mrs. Louise Walters, a white woman, who told the most fantastic of the stories about the drowning. Mrs. Walters described herself as "a former hoodoo queen and professional card reader."

"I was one of the best in the work," she said, "but I gave up hoodoo to please my daughter. She has modern ideas, so now we're all Baptists.

"I sure used to make a lot of money. You see I learned what I know from Marie Laveau, and she was the best in the world. It sure was funny how I met her. One day when

I was a young girl I went out by Bayou St. John to catch some crawfish. It was exactly three days after the St. John's Eve storm. It was all over town that Marie Laveau was drowned, but I didn't know much about her and so I didn't pay it much mind.

"Well, I come to a place where some trees was sort of bunched together near the edge of the water and to my surprise I saw a woman lying across a box. She was soaking wet and looked like she was dead. I was sure scared, but I went closer and looked at her good. She had on a brown dress and a blue veil over her face. All of a sudden I heard her moan, so I bent down and spoke to her. Then her eyes opened up. She looked straight into my face and, let me tell you, I never saw such eyes. They were beautiful and they went straight through you. Her lips moved and she said, 'Help me, child.'

"I got her to sitting up and at last she was on her feet with one arm around my shoulders. 'Take me home with you,' she said. 'I've got to have some coffee and some dry clothes. No one must see me like this.' We was sitting in my mother's kitchen before she told me who she was. First, she asked my mother to leave the room, then she said, very quiet-like, 'I love you, my child, and I don't love many people. I am Marie Laveau.' I'll tell you I began to shake, I was that scared. 'But they say you're dead,' I told her. 'I know,' she said. 'Marie Laveau's been dead before.' Wasn't that a funny thing for her to say? And then she started laughing, and she said, 'I'm a strong woman. You come see me sometime.'

"After that we was good friends. I went to see her in that white cabin she had all the time, and she would come see me. She taught me a lot of her secrets. But about two years after that she disappeared. God knows what become of her. She was a strange woman and a great mystic. I never did hear of her dying."

So it goes. The ideas regarding the date of her death can

be carried to almost absurd extremes. For instance, Christine Harris said, "She lived until 1918. I is sure of that 'cause it was after the big war when she died. She was still holdin' meetin's and she was still dancin'. One day she was dancin' and she stop and look up at the sky and started screamin'. Then she fell down. She was dead, and the devil had her for his own."

If that is true she was 91, and her dancing must have been remarkable. Christine had her confused with a later Voodooienne. Several probably borrowed the name of Marie Laveau.

August Augustine told a story that was entirely different from any of the others. August said he attended a masquerade ball in the Globe Hall, a building on St. Claude Street near St. Peter Street. Downstairs was the headquarters of a colored Masonic lodge and upstairs there were rooms that were sometimes rented for dances, political meetings and other affairs. This particular ball, August said, was during the Mardi Gras season of 1897. Marie came late in the evening and dressed as she always dressed, while everyone else was in costume, but, despite this, she attracted more attention than anyone else there. He added that she had become very stout and weighed well over two hundred pounds.

The ball was nearly over when Marie decided to leave. She was halfway down the stairs when she collapsed and she fell the rest of the way. When a doctor present reached her she was dead. "It was her heart," August said. "It was all over in a minute. That is really the way death came to Marie Laveau. All them other stories ain't true. She was buried in the Basin Street graveyard they call St. Louis No. I, and she was put in the same tomb with her mother and the rest of her family. She had a big funeral because she belonged to the Society of the Ladies with Tignons and the Society of the Ladies of La Pousiniere. Right after she died them societies broke up."

There is an inscription on the Laveau-Glapion tomb in St. Louis Cemetery No. 1 that may—and certainly should—indicate that this is the resting place of Marie II. The tomb is white and has three crypts with a "receiving vault" beneath to hold the remains of other people when they must be moved to make room for a new burial. Here lie the Widow Paris—though none of the three slabs indicates the presence of her remains—and her common-law husband, Christophe Glapion. Probably there was once an inscription marking the vault in which the first Marie Laveau was buried, but it has been changed for one marking a later burial. The bones of the Widow Paris must lie in the receiving vault below. However, the middle slab reads:

> *Famille Vve Paris*
> *née Laveau*
> *Ci—Gît*
> *Marie Philome Glapion,*
> *décédée le 11 Juin 1897,*
> *Âgée de Soixante-deux ans Elle fut*
> *bonne mère, bonne amie, et*
> *regrettée par tous ceux qui l'ont*
> *connue Passante priez pour elle.*

A great many Voodoos accept this vault as the burial place of the Marie Laveau they remember—Marie II—and they come here to knock three times on the slab and ask a favor. They bring flowers and sometimes burn candles here and leave pennies and nickels in the green flower-holders that are attached to each side of the tomb. There are always penciled crosses on the slab. The sexton washes the crosses away, but they always reappear. It is possible that some of those persons who come here do so because they know this is the burial place of the Widow Paris; however most of them know nothing of her and are seeking favors of Marie II.

There is an even larger group of those who do not accept

this as her resting place at all. Where she is buried has become
a highly controversial matter that has grown out of all proportion to its importance. Yet it is vital to the Voodoos. The
grave of Marie Laveau should be a shrine. You can find as
many opinions on the subject as there are cemeteries in New
Orleans.

The argument that she is not buried in the Laveau tomb
is based, of course, on the fact that she was exiled from the
family by Madame Legendre. "Old Madame Legendre
wouldn't have nothin' to do wit' her even when she died,"
said Théophile Miche, who recalled Marie II well. "The
writin' on that slab ain't her. That's another sister. You know
in them days people might name three or four daughters
'Marie,' like one would be 'Marie Rose,' another 'Marie The-
resa,' and another 'Marie Louisa.' That was an old Creole
custom. Marie Laveau died of old age in 1901 and she is
buried in St. Louis Cemetery No. 2. People who goes to
that place in St. Louis No. 1 is crazy."

Yet many keep coming to that tomb. It is always main-
tained in perfect condition, its exterior being whitewashed
several times a year and the flower-holders given a coat of
green paint. The sexton did not know who took care of it,
said Théophile. Perhaps he did not want to say. He will tell
you only that "lots of people come," and that on such occasions as All Saints' Day the tomb is decorated with bouquets
of fresh flowers. Other things appear, too; bits of wax twisted
into grotesque shapes are dropped into the flower-holders;
sometimes a rosary is found hanging on that middle slab;
once he found a full set of false teeth!

There is also a "Marie Laveau Tomb" in the cemetery
known as St. Louis No. 2. This is not really a tomb at all,
but one crypt among the many that form the wall encircling
the cemetery. These crypts are known in New Orleans as
"ovens," and are a very old and typical kind of burial place.

Because until recent years ground burials were impossible in New Orleans these crypts were necessary to hold the remains of poor persons who could not afford an entire tomb. They built one on top of the other, usually about four of them, and the earliest ones each have a rounded top which accounts for their resemblance to ovens. They can even be rented and should the family fail to meet the rent the remains are removed and burned.

The "oven" in which some persons believe Marie II to have been buried is at the rear of the cemetery. Its slab is always covered with literally hundreds of crosses made with red brick. Until recently there was a crack in the slab, and into this devotees would drop coins and then make a wish. There was a particular belief that here any girl wishing a husband could be certain of having her desire fulfilled. The rite consists of rapping on the slab three times, saying the wish out loud, then making a cross with red brick, a piece of which always reposes on top of the row of crypts. This place is also known as the "Wishing Vault" and the "Voodoo Vault," and probably more Voodoos will accept it as the burial place of Marie Laveau than they will the tomb in St. Louis Cemetery No. 1.

However, others will tell you that this is a mistake, and that another Voodoo queen, Marie Comtesse, is buried here, that in some way the two became confused. The sexton will tell you that "there ain't nothing in that oven but some old bones of people what died of Yellow Fever. I don't know how this started, but they keep coming—white and colored—and making their crosses. It's a damned nuisance."

There are many other beliefs as to where Marie Laveau lies, including Girod Street Cemetery, Louisa Street Cemetery, and Holt Cemetery, and each person has great confidence that he is correct.

Jimmie St. Clair, colored, believed the body had been buried originally in the Laveau tomb and was later moved, and that this is what started the confusion.

"She was in St. Louis No. 1," he said, "but her spirit wouldn't behave. Everybody got so scared they wouldn't go near the cemetery, and that was bad for business. She used to appear in the shape of one of them big Newfoundland dogs. Madame Legendre and the other relatives got ashamed—you know how stuck up they was—so they moved her to Holt Cemetery and buried her there without no mark on her grave. They just put a block of cement over the ground, and that kept her. They left the name off because they wanted people to forget her. That's a laugh, huh? People around this town never will forget Marie Laveau."

Elmore Lee Banks, also colored, thought he had good reason to believe this was not true and that Marie still reposed in the St. Louis Cemetery No. 1 tomb.

"I was in a drugstore right near St. Louis No. 1 one day," he said, "and this wasn't no more than ten years ago. An old woman dressed in a long white dress and with a blue *tignon* come in and stood right next to me. I didn't pay her no mind, but kept on explaining to the drugstore man what I wanted. All of a sudden I notice he wasn't listening to me at all, but was looking at this old woman and his eyes was popping out his head like a frog's. Before I knowed what had happened he turned around and ran like a fool into the back of his store.

"I didn't know what to do, so I turned around and looked at this woman. She looked back at me, and she start laughing kind of like she was crazy. She just laughed and laughed and, me, I thought she was just some poor crazy woman that the druggist was scared of. God, if I'd known what was coming I'd have died on the spot!

"Well, she kept laughing a while, then she say, 'Don't you know me?' I say, 'No, ma'am.' Then I say, 'Where the drugstore man go at?' That seem to make her mad. Her eyes got like fire and she picked up one of her hands and smacked me right in the face. Then she jump up in the air and went whizzing out the door and over the top of the telephone wires. She passed right over the graveyard wall and disappeared. Then I passed out cold.

"When I woke up the drugstore man was pouring whiskey down my throat. 'You know who that was?' he ask me. I couldn't talk yet. 'That was Marie Laveau,' he say. 'She been dead for years and years, but every once in a while people around here see her. Son, you is been slapped by the Queen of the Voodoos!' "

# 16
# The Power Divided

"MARIE LAVEAU is dead! Malvina Latour is queen!"

That was the announcement made by all the New Orleans newspapers when the Widow Paris died in 1881. Marie II remained the leading Voodoo figure, but it was Malvina Latour who reigned as official ruler of the St. John's Eve celebrations for the next decade.

We do not actually know a great deal about Malvina Latour. There is a physical description of a heavy-set woman in her forties. She was much darker than either of the Laveaus. It has been said that she was the daughter of Marie II, probably by a Negro man. This is without evidence. When he saw her Cable wrote of "a bright mulattress of about forty-eight, of extremely handsome figure, dignified bearing, and a face indicative of a comparatively high order of intelligence." It has been said that her brother was a member of the infamous black-and-tan Legislature. She was at times confused with the Laveaus and was frequently referred to as "Marie Laveau," thus becoming in a sense a sort of Marie III, though probably with no intention of doing so.

Despite the Marie Laveau still living, Malvina seems to have had a strong will and a mind of her own. She held the St. John's Eve gatherings in the traditional fashion and is said to have been a striking figure in dresses of blue calico with white dots and handsome scarlet and orange *tignons*. One of her first acts was an attempt to remove Catholicism and Catholic practices from Voodoo, though, since the two are still mingled today, she was evidently not very successful.

She was a Catholic, herself, and said she practiced Voodooism as a profession, not as a religion, and, inconsistent as it seems, was given to expressing the opinion that such misuse of the Roman Catholic ritual and symbols was sacrilegious.

She had been a part of the Voodoo world for many years, had substituted for Marie II at many ceremonies and was building a clientele of her own even before her appointment as ruler. In 1870, in a crowded Negro church, she is reported to have performed a miraculous cure upon the preacher, a Reverend Turner, who was suffering from an incurable ailment. Seekers after health and money and love came to her home just as they had come to the Laveaus, though she was never anywhere near as well known.

But in general her practices duplicated the Laveaus', and it is doubtful that she created any new *gris-gris* of importance. She inspired the same fears, to a lesser degree. Numerous persons who remember her tell of wrecked homes and Voodoo murders. "Malvina Latour was the worst of them all," said Irma Lee Richards. She was not that. She was only an imitator. New Orleans knew the end of a colorful era was signaled by the death of the Widow Paris. The *Times Democrat* had said then: "Much evil dies with her, but should we not add, a little poetry?" Perhaps that is the reason Malvina Latour did not rise to the heights of the Laveaus. She did not have the poetry.

As the years passed Madame Legendre fought with increasing vigor to remove the Voodoo stigma from the Laveau ménage. Years after the death of the Widow Paris, Mrs. Walter Saxon called on Madame and asked permission to do a painting of the house. This was granted, and Madame Legendre seems to have treated her quite graciously. "It is such a relief to have someone here who doesn't ask questions and make rude remarks," said Madame. "So many people come here and ask if this is where 'that awful old Voodoo lived'! Do you realize they are speaking of my mother? My mother was a saint—a most devout Catholic; all of us are good Catholics."

In 1903 the little cottage was razed. Today nothing remains but that small painting of it which is now the property of Mrs. Helen Pitkin Schertz, author of a novel with a Voodoo background and entitled *An Angel By Brevet*.

It is fairly certain that there are no authentic portraits of either of the Laveaus, though there are several that are claimed as such. The most notable of these is the George W. Catlin portrait, formerly in the Louisiana State Museum at the Cabildo in New Orleans. As the picture is dated 1835, the woman could be the Widow Paris, but this is extremely doubtful. Madame Legendre and other members of the family always insisted that no painting or photograph had ever been made of the mother. In 1942 whispers spread through the Voodoo grapevine that Father Divine had offered to pay $5,000 for the Catlin portrait. He wanted to hang Marie Laveau in "Heaven."

After the passing of the Laveaus, Voodoo in New Orleans split into many parts and there were even more leaders than there had ever been before Marie I had bound them together under her powerful direction. Malvina Latour did not succeed in keeping the cult intact, and by the 1890's she was not ruling all the Voodoos in the city, but only a sect of her own, though it probably remained the largest and most important of them all.

Marie II had allowed many persons to work with her and had taught many of them her secrets, and some of the surviving associates formed their own groups and set themselves up in their own businesses.

A Negro named Léon Janpier is well remembered. He had lived in the Laveau cottage for a time and was rumored to have been a lover of Marie II. Each day, for years, Léon Janpier went to St. Louis Cemetery No. 1 and "made the four corners." This is a curious rite still practiced. The person performing it enters the cemetery and goes to each corner in turn, bowing as he reaches each one and making a wish. Then he departs hurriedly and walks two blocks to the Church of Our Lady of Guadalupe on North Rampart Street and says a prayer before the statue of St. Expédite.

"Léon Janpier was the best graveyard worker Marie Laveau had," said Octave Labeau, who claimed to be a relative of the great Maries, despite the difference in the spelling of their names. This he explained by saying that "sometimes names gits mixed up. The old people didn't know how to spell and parts of the family spelled it different from other parts. But Marie Laveau was my great-aunt and she was a wonderful woman. I used to see her every day when she and Léon Janpier would go to the graveyard.

"I remember Miss Jackson, too. She was sure good. She learned her stuff workin' wit' Marie Laveau and Janpier. She was a big black woman and she used to give hoodoo dances at her house on Roman Street. She would stand in the middle of the floor and clap her hands while the people danced around her. They killed a rooster and drank blood and everything. She had her a snake and she sold liquor to the people what came. Nobody couldn't bring in no liquor from outside. They had to buy hers. She knew how to run a Voodoo business." Octave Labeau also recalled Madame Joyeau, Madame Titite and a white queen known as Madame Auguste.

Madame Auguste is supposed to have been very tall and beautiful when young and to have danced at the Laveau meetings. After Marie II was gone she held together a large cult of her own, drawing to it many white persons who preferred working under a white queen rather than a colored one. About 1895 she vanished into obscurity. In her old age she

lost all her former beauty and is said to have been somewhat
terrifying in appearance and to have lost an eye. The latter
greatly increased her prestige for people credited the one
fierce orb with supernatural powers.

Another Voodooienne, Angèle Levasseur, apparently went
too far in imitating Marie Laveau. While she was holding a
meeting in her cabin near Lake Pontchartrain in 1894 a storm
swept the shack away with Angèle inside. She was found
three days later, sitting on the limb of a tree floating on the
surface of the water. On the other hand, perhaps this was
not an imitation of Marie, but the real origin of the Laveau
story of drowning. In any case it is Angèle's only claim to
distinction and all we know about her.

For some unknown reason all the Voodoo queens seem
to be given to floating around on lakes, canals and bayous
for days on end. Clare Scott told the story of Mamie Hughes,
who was, according to Clare, "the worst damn old hoodoo
what ever lived."

"She killed her own sister's baby and kept its skeleton in
her house," Clare said, shivering and rolling her black eyes
dramatically. "She ate little children and played with turtles
and rattlesnakes that still had poison in 'em.

"One day old Mamie fell in the Orleans Canal and floated
around for nearly a week. She was almost passing out when
Chinee Frank came along and dragged her in. Chinee Frank
was a good man what lived on Villeré Street. He took her
home and rolled the water out of her. The poor man brought
evil back into the world without knowing what he was doing. But she never got out of her bed again. Her heart was
so hard the water had started to rot it away. I went to see
her and there was polices all over the place. They was gonna
hang her as soon as she was strong enough to stand it. A
thousand people stood day and night around that house, waiting and hoping she'd get well enough to hang. It was too

late. Her heart was all rotted and she was dying. She done broke down and confessed all her sins, and the polices found skeletons of babies all over the house and buried in the back yard. One woman was standing by her bed and all of a sudden she say, 'What's them two lumps on her head?' Everybody look and sure enough there was two horns starting to grow out of her. She belonged to the devil. Everybody's done heard how she screamed and hollered when she heard the chariots coming from hell. Next thing she know she was dead."

Clare also remembered Marie Comtesse, who was, apparently, an entirely different type. She was of the opinion that it was "La Comtesse," as she called her, who was buried in the Wishing Vault in St. Louis Cemetery No. 2.

"La Comtesse was a big black woman and she was married to a nice-looking, light fellow," Clare said. "She had two daughters. I'm sure she is the one buried in the Wishing Vault, not Marie Laveau. Peoples get all mixed up. I knows all about it—even how she died. She was standing on her gallery, leaning against a post, and the post give way and she fell and broke her neck. Poor La Comtesse! I tell you the truth, I sure loved her. I goes to her place in the graveyard and I brings her apples. She always liked apples."

Clare gave a detailed description of La Comtesse, who she said was five feet, three inches tall and weighed about two hundred pounds. "She had the biggest eyes I ever seen. You keep looking at 'em a few minutes and you is hoodooed. She had a crowded house and she made lots of money."

Marie Comtesse went about the city a great deal and she had many contacts inside the homes of white people. Unlike Marie Laveau, she often went to a client's home to render certain services. Her costume for what Clare called her "traveling trade" was quite different from that which she wore at her meetings. To bless homes and rid them of evil she wore a long purple dress with a red headdress. She carried a small leather satchel that contained her *gris-gris* and other paraphernalia. Sometimes she carried a white velvet bag instead of the satchel.

While conducting her services she wore many gowns, changing them often during the same night, as an actress changes costumes in a play. She would, for instance, begin the ceremonies in a black velvet robe, change to one of scarlet satin, then close the ceremonies wearing a gown of white chiffon with voluminous sleeves. An excellent showwoman, but lacking the personal appeal of the Laveaus, she invented numerous stunts to add to the interest of her gatherings. One trick was to fill her rooms with shapely young mulatto girls, who danced and sang in very brief costumes, and sometimes, Clare said, entirely without clothing.

"The mens loved her services," Clare said. "They'd whirl the womens on their backs the way hoodoos always do and everybody whoop and holler and have a fine old time.

"There's one thing always bothers me. La Comtesse made plenty of money, but nobody has ever knowed what she done with it. Now it was different with Marie Laveau. I been told she left two million dollars buried out in the swamps around Bayou St. John; I can remember one time when Doctor Alexander went out there and tried to find it. But all that ain't true. Marie Laveau was a awful gambler. It's true she gived a lot away, but most of it she lost gambling. It was different with La Comtesse. She didn't gamble. She might have gived it all away. She was that good."

Clare was slow to admit it, but at last she confessed she had used young girls as bait when she was conducting her own Voodoo business, some twenty years ago. "I learned that from La Comtesse," she said, "but I had to give it up. It sure did draw the trade, but it drawed the polices, too, and that don't do you no good."

Marie Brown is the great-granddaughter of a Voodoo queen of the Widow Paris period. Marie at first refused to discuss Queen Eliza at all. "I ain't tellin' my secrets to nobody," she said. However, a little later she began to boast of her ancestress and was soon enjoying herself tremendously.

"My great-grandma was named by Marie Saloppé," she said. "Her own mother had come from Santo Domingo and they was all hoodoo people. When my great-grandma was borned Marie Saloppé called her 'Eliza,' and she grew up to be a big hoodoo queen herself and was known as 'Queen Eliza of the Dance.' She danced at all the Marie Laveau meetin's on St. John's Eve. One thing she could do was to put a glass of water on her head and dance wit'out spillin' a drop. Sometimes she would dance wit' a lighted candle on her head.

"She used to wrap her legs wit' ribbons and she'd have a big red bow on each knee. Madras handkerchiefs used to cost five dollars each then, but that wasn't nothin' to Queen Eliza of the Dance. She wore ten of 'em for a skirt.

"Besides the hoodoo dances, the firemans always had her at their balls and one time when she couldn't go they called off a big ball just on her account. She was wonderful, my grandma always told me. You know what she called my grandma when she was borned? She called her 'Three Cents.' That was a hoodoo name. My grandma went by that name all her life. She was named like that 'cause when Queen Eliza was gonna have her she was always eatin' ginger cake, and ginger cake cost three cents. My grandma sure was proud of that name—Three Cents Wilden. But I'll tell you a funny thing: my grandma never was a hoodoo. Her and my mamma was Catholic to the backbone." Marie said that she was a Baptist herself, but that in her younger days she had "messed wit' hoodoo a little, but then I turned against it."

"Queen Eliza didn't do any real evil work," Marie contended, "but she sure had people scared of her. She used to drink black cat's blood and that give her lots of *power*. She was wild."

Marie had known some of the later queens, who were important in her own lifetime. She had known both Marie Comtesse and Mamie Hughes.

"Right now there is more hoodoo around this town than there ever was," said Marie. "But it sure has changed. I'll say this, though: it's a good thing to keep away from. It has just as much *power* over the people now as it ever did, and it can do some funny things. Hoodoo is somethin' people shouldn't even talk about. It might be changed, but it's just as bad as it ever was."

Marie was at least partially right. After the turn of the century Voodoo had changed and had fallen into segments. In a way it resembled the fragments of a wineglass that had been smashed into many pieces. But there was just as much glass.

# 17
# Love Story

UNTIL the spring of 1944 a withered, shawl-wrapped hag came to beg for food at the back doors of houses in the neighborhood of St. Ann and North Rampart Streets in New Orleans. Sometimes she stopped passersby in the streets and held out a hand like a crushed leaf. Sometimes she was seen at dawn kneeling in the center aisle of Our Lady of Guadalupe Church, a rosary tangled in her crooked fingers.

Whenever they saw her the people of that section of the city would begin to tell of her history, and the listeners could not help wondering what voluptuous memories must sometimes creep through the crevices of her aged mind, like the young tendrils of the green ferns that are always fighting their way through the cracks in the decaying tombs in old New Orleans cemeteries.

Euphrasine Tabouis was the only child of a jeweler who kept a shop in Royal Street. Her mother had died at her birth and she and her father lived quietly, but not unhappily, in living quarters above his place of business. During the day Euphrasine went to school with the sisters at the convent and in the evenings she read to her father, while he dozed beside the fire in their neat parlor, or sewed and chattered away of the day's adventures—of how some wicked girl had placed a huge green frog in Sister Marguerite's desk or of how exciting it was that Georgette Ducoyeille was already engaged to be married, and before she was sixteen!

It was the summer that Euphrasine was fifteen that the doctor told Monsieur Tabouis the truth about his heart. It

would not be very long before the end of these peaceful evenings would come and Euphrasine would be alone. He said
nothing to the girl, but grieved secretly. It was not good that
such a tender creature should be left so alone. Besides, New
Orleans was a wicked city, filled with temptations. M. Tabouis
knew of only one solution. Before he died his daughter must
be safely married.

The distracted father thought that surely God had answered
his prayers when, just a few weeks after receiving the doctor's
verdict, one Monsieur Pigeon, a recent arrival from Paris and
a watchmaker by trade, appeared in the shop seeking employ-
ment. Jules Pigeon was hired immediately—as soon as Tabouis
had ascertained that he was a bachelor—and was invited to
make his home in the apartment upstairs.

The father did not wait long to approach the Frenchman
regarding what was uppermost in his mind. One evening, after
Euphrasine had retired, the two men sat before the fire sip-
ping bourbon and water, while Tabouis told of his fears, at
last frankly suggesting that Jules marry his daughter. "All
this," he said, waving a hand to indicate the shop, the living
quarters, his whole world, "will then be yours. In return I
ask only that you cherish and protect my little Euphrasine
all the days of your life together."

Jules was stunned, but he agreed almost at once. The truth
was that he had been almost mad with love for the girl from
the first moment he had set eyes upon her. With her creamy
skin and dark eyes and great mass of curling jet hair, she was,
despite her youth, the most beautiful woman he had ever seen
in his life. "She is like one of these Louisiana magnolias," he
had written a friend in Paris.

When they told her, Euphrasine turned very pale, but consented immediately. Then she went to weep in her room. She
did not love Jules Pigeon. He was very gentle and kind, but
he was so old—thirty-six, a middle-aged man!—and he was

so peculiar looking. She knew how the urchins in the neighborhood made fun of him. They said he looked exactly like his name; they even made it diminutive because of his lack of height, and to be more insulting. "Monsieur le Pigeonneau!" they called after him in Royal Street. "Monsieur le Squab!" Even the girls at the convent teased her by inquiring, "How is Monsieur le Squab?" And now she was to marry him.

No time was wasted. Two weeks after it had been arranged Euphrasine and Jules Pigeon were married. A month later Monsieur Tabouis passed away in his sleep.

Though she knew she could never love him, Euphrasine was a well reared Creole girl, so she tried to like and respect her husband; but as the months passed she found this increasingly difficult. Jules' passion for her grew more and more intense and every day his caresses became even more repulsive. She began to discover that he was her slave, not the master a husband should be, and soon she was treating him with indifference and with contempt. Sometimes she would catch herself thinking, "Monsieur le Squab! Madame la Squab!" At first she was ashamed of her feelings. Then she no longer cared.

Euphrasine had enjoyed none of her youth. Except that she had a husband now instead of a father, her life was almost unchanged. Jules was tired in the evenings. He liked to doze by the fire, with his belt loosened after a huge supper, while she read to him just as she had done for her father. She had not even the convent to go to now. Besides, when her young married friends invited them out Jules did not care to go. He did not dance and he did not care for the theater, and parties bored him. At last she began to go out without him, and he, after seeing that she was properly chaperoned, did not seem to mind. When she returned from a *soirée*, still excited and gay, her eyes and cheeks bright with laughter and wine, he would be in bed snoring. And he snored very loudly.

They had been married over a year when Euphrasine was invited to go to a Voodoo meeting. She was attending a large party on St. John's Eve when someone present, remembering the date, suggested that they all go, and everyone agreed instantly. Euphrasine had heard of Voodoo all her life, had even been thrilled at the sight of Marie Laveau, sweeping down Royal Street, with a crowd of her people following her, and the idea of seeing a real ceremony delighted her, so she was one of the first to support the idea. An hour before midnight the entire crowd climbed into carriages and set out for the wilderness edging Bayou St. John.

When they reached their destination they found a scene as wild as any they had imagined. Flares and torches circled a cleared space where the Voodoos were gathered. In the center a tall woman in a *tignon* clapped her hands and screamed instructions to the devotees. A great mass of nearly naked blacks—with a few white bodies here and there— danced and gyrated about her, chanting and answering the cries of their queen. In the background someone beat an ass's thighbone on a deerskin stretched taut over a beer keg.

Most of the women wanted to go home and some of the men were disgusted, but Euphrasine crept as close as she dared. The beat of the tom-tom seemed to be her own heart-beat, and the flames of the torches fired her blood. She felt as if she had suddenly opened a door and walked into another life.

Then something happened. The beating of the drum ceased, the dancers sprawled on the ground on their faces and there was such a silence that the watchers could hear the mosquitoes singing in their ears. Out into the clearing whirled a man.

Euphrasine had never seen such a man. He was well over six feet tall, with a slender waist and a torso of rippling muscle, while his legs had the symmetry of a ballet dancer.

He wore a red madras handkerchief about his loins and the rest of his body glowed in the firelight as if he were carved out of pure gold. On one ankle a ring of tiny bells tinkled as he danced. On one ear something gleamed—a great ornament of living jewels.

And how he danced! Whirling and leaping into the air, spinning on his toes so fast it made the spectators dizzy to watch him, striking obscene, almost impossible, postures, trembling and quivering as if currents of electricity were passing through his body. "Who is that?" one of the women asked. "Prince Basile," answered a man. "Just a quadroon witch doctor." Another man said hastily, "I think we should go."

But Euphrasine drew her cape about her, turned away from her friends and walked straight into the brush circling the clearing.

They called after her, but she didn't answer. Then they spent more than an hour searching for her. The torches went out and the Voodoos began to disband. At last, the women hysterical, the men puzzled and shocked, they all rode slowly back toward the city. They were never to see Euphrasine Pigeon again.

It is said that when they told Jules, poor Monsieur le Squab fell to the floor, striking his head, and was unconscious for two days. When he recovered he summoned the police and a relentless search was begun. The officers even went to the home of Marie Laveau. She vowed she knew nothing of the girl. Many young ladies came to view her "harmless and entirely religious" ceremonies these days. Prince Basile was mentioned, but only casually, since there was no reason to connect him with the disappearance of Madame Pigeon. Finally the police notified Jules that they were of the opinion that his wife had probably in some way fallen into Bayou St. John and been drowned.

Jules did not believe this, but there was nothing else to do.

As weeks extended into months he grieved more and more. He became a silent man who spoke only when he was first addressed, and his hair grayed. Each morning and evening he went to pray at the Cathedral and each night he sat late before the fire in his parlor weeping into his hands.

But Euphrasine was not dead. When she left her friends she had remained close to the edge of the clearing, walking through the trees until she came to the place where Prince Basile had entered the area. Here she concealed herself in the shadows and waited, trembling and scarcely conscious of what she was doing, until, with a magnificent gesture, Prince Basile swept aside the brush and passed but a few inches from her. Then she spoke to him and he came close, gazing down into her upturned face. No one knows what she said or what he replied, but when he left the orgy she went with him.

Prince Basile—his real name was Joseph Howard, and he was a quadroon from Gretna, just across the Mississippi River from New Orleans—lived in a one-room shack near Lake Pontchartrain, a dirty, almost unfurnished hut. On a shelf built against one wall were some skulls and half-burned candles. In one corner a pile of old and filthy quilts served as a bed. In another a charcoal furnace served for heat and cooking. It has been said that the night he brought home Euphrasine there was a mulatto woman there and that he threw her out bodily and installed Euphrasine as his new concubine.

It is also said the girl, despite the poverty and dirt, despite the savage brutality of her lover, was deliriously happy for the next few months. Nowadays we would delve into Freud to understand Euphrasine. It is probable that she was a highly sensual woman with some abnormal tendencies, perhaps edging on nymphomania. But whatever it was, nights in the arms of Prince Basile on that loathsome bed of quilts compensated for and were more important to her than the mere comfort and middle-class security of the establishment in Royal Street and the kindness of Monsieur Pigeon.

But Prince Basile changed his woman often. This white one was a novelty, but he had no intention of keeping her forever. He took great delight in beating and torturing her. He would use his fists upon her. He would pull her long hair until she screamed in agony. Sometimes he scratched her white body with his nails or bit her tender breasts until the blood flowed. The *pièce de résistance* of this tale is that he would sometimes bend over her as if to kiss her throat or her breasts, then, quickly turning his head, he would scratch her horribly with the jagged ornament of jewels that never left his right ear. Euphrasine must have been cursed with masochism that matched his sadism, for none of this lessened her passion for the Voodoo dancer. On the other hand, perhaps she was bewitched—perhaps she was *fixed*.

It lasted a year. At the end of that time, on the next St. John's Eve, Prince Basile brought home a buxom, coal-black Negress and told Euphrasine to leave the shack. We are told that she fell to her knees and begged him to keep her, but that he and the Negress beat her and drove her away.

No one knows exactly what happened in the interim, but a few weeks later Euphrasine Pigeon appeared in a house of prostitution located on Basin Street, in that notorious section of the city known as "Storyville." Perhaps, feeling that there was nowhere else to go, she had knocked at the door of the place the very night that her quadroon lover had dismissed her, and that the "Madame," seeing her potentialities, had taken her in and kept her hidden away until she had recovered from the marks which a year with Prince Basile must have left upon her. We must remember that she was only seventeen and that youth recuperates quickly. In any case, she was introduced to Storyville as "Lottie" and as having recently arrived from Vienna, and she was soon the most popular girl in the house.

The bagnios of the New Orleans of that period were unbelievably luxurious. There were elegant drawing rooms in which "guests" were received, filled with fine black walnut and mahogany pieces, thick Oriental rugs and oil paintings and ornate mirrors. The boudoirs occupied by the girls were equally sumptuous. In the more expensive establishments only gentlemen in evening clothes were admitted, and they were received by the ladies in handsome and costly evening gowns. Champagne and the finest foods were served. Most of the houses offered music and other entertainment apart from their principal type of business. Gentlemen could come to call and spend an evening dancing. If one desired to spend the night he would choose his girl and be escorted to a splendid bedchamber with walls of tufted satin or mirrors. In the morning breakfast would be served.

For nearly two years "Lottie" was the reigning beauty of the house in which she worked. She had many assets besides her beauty and sensuality. She had a charming voice and would occasionally entertain guests by singing, while another girl accompanied her at the piano. She had an educated speaking voice and an air of refinement that gave her clients the illusion that she was anything but a prostitute available to any man who had the price. Several men fell in love with her, and she received expensive gifts of clothing and jewelry wholly apart from her usual fees. She was not unhappy. She had no distaste for the life, and everything that was sordid or unpleasant was kept outside the hand-carved mahogany front doors. Only one thing bothered her. She kept dreaming of her Voodoo lover.

There is no way we can know now, but her decision to visit the witch doctor must have come after a long battle within herself and the decisive moment must have arrived with that same characteristic impulsiveness which had caused her to forsake her former respectable life the night of the Voodoo meeting. One summer evening, complaining of a headache from the heat, she retired to her room and bedecked herself in the most captivating of her finery. When she was dressed she covered her face with a heavy veil and left the house by a rear exit in order to avoid the gay crowd in the rooms to the front of the house. Outside a rented carriage awaited, and soon she was following the winding course of Bayou St. John. This was to be a great triumph!

She dismissed the carriage when the familiar outline of the shack was in sight, and went the rest of the way on foot. As she approached she called his name. The door of the hut opened, and Prince Basile came toward her in the moonlight. He was probably simple enough to be impressed for a while. At any rate, he welcomed her with passion and soon she was inside the shack. She was gratified to find no woman there, and she must have decided with feminine logic that after all he had been grieving for her and had come to a realization that he could love no woman but her. Accordingly she played the great lady, flashing her jewels in the candlelight and making him beg and plead before she yielded herself to him.

Toward morning she awoke from a heavy sleep, crawled out of his still-encircling arms and shook him roughly so that he would awaken. Now she was seized with sudden hatred for this man who had been so long a fixation. She must have recalled his cruelties, most of all how he had driven her away that night to put a black woman in her place. With narrowed eyes she studied his powerful, cream-colored body, then his face with the thick, faintly Negroid features and the jeweled earring gleaming from that right ear.

She began to pour forth a torrent of abuse. She called him names, cursed him in language learned in Storyville, laughed scornfully, called him a "nigger." At last she stopped to catch her breath. His face was without emotion, mysterious and impassive. He had said not a word in reply. She was almost disappointed that he did not fall upon her and beat her as he had done before. Now she felt that he was her slave, that he had become like Monsieur le Squab. She rose and began to put on her clothes, continuing to revile and insult him. When she was nearly dressed she turned and spat in his face, then laughed contemptuously, for he still said not a word. Then she extended a naked foot, a small, white, very pretty foot, and demanded that he kiss it.

Prince Basile fell to his knees before her and took her ankle between his hands. He bent low over the foot and Euphrasine raised her black brows, waiting in a sort of ecstasy for his kiss. But the quadroon did not touch the slender arch with his thick red lips. Instead, he turned his head quickly and the jagged ear-ornament stabbed into her sensitive flesh. With another swift movement of his head he slashed open the foot from ankle to toes. Then he stood up, raised a hand and slapped her in the mouth with his open palm.

They say it was three days later that Euphrasine wandered into the Royal Street shop of Monsieur Pigeon. He was alone, working at his bench, when he looked up and saw a woman, her clothing in tatters, her hair disheveled and her face covered with blood and dirt. With a cry of delight he gathered his Euphrasine up in his arms, as if she had been a child, and carried her quickly to the rooms upstairs. It is an important part of this story that as he climbed the stairs he is supposed to have said over and over, "Marie Laveau brought you back to me! Marie Laveau brought you back to me!" For, when his prayers at the Cathedral were unanswered, Jules had at last gone to the cottage of Marie Laveau and asked her help. Her opinion had been that his wife was somewhere suffering under a curse, which could be removed and the girl returned for a fee of a thousand dollars. Jules is supposed to have paid this price. Now she had come home.

It is also said that while he washed the filth of her three days of wandering from her body and combed the tangles from her beautiful hair, he whispered no words other than those of affection and thanksgiving that she had returned. Whatever wonderment went through his mind as to her whereabouts during the three years was not expressed. She spoke not a word.

It happened when poor Jules began to bathe her injured foot. He cleansed the gash tenderly, applied medicines of some sort and began to bandage it. Then he is supposed to have cried, "Oh, my dearest, the cobblestones have cut your little foot terribly!" The girl burst into insane laughter and screamed, "Monsieur le Squab! Monsieur le Pigeonneau!" Then she fainted.

During the years that followed no one ever saw Madame Pigeon. Gossip said she was quite mad and that her husband kept her locked in a room above the shop. Jules lived to be very old. It was nearly forty years later when he died and that Madame Pigeon appeared on the streets of New Orleans. All her beauty had long been gone, and she was already a hag. Her funds vanished, and she became a street character and a beggar.

She never spoke to anyone except to ask for food, and if she were asked a question she would answer in as few words as possible. It was impossible to determine how sane she was or what was in her mind. Once she was asked about Marie Laveau.

"Marie Laveau was a big Voodoo," she said. "That's all I know. I wish people would talk to me in French. I don't know English so good."

Euphrasine had been speaking English all her life.

# Part III
## THIS IS
## THE WAY IT IS

# 18
# You Gotta Be Opened

MADAME CAZAUNOUX was in a drinking mood. She demanded both wine and beer, not only for herself, but also for Madame Jean and Gaston Fontaine, who are spirits and without whom Madame insisted she could not be one of the current Voodoo queens of New Orleans.

When the wine and beer were brought she mixed the two together and set out three separate tall tumblers of the concoction on the table beside her rocker. She drained one quickly, then picked up another. "Ah, Mimmie, next time I will give you whiskey," she promised an invisible personage, and drank about half of the contents of that glass.

Madame, very small, stooped and probably a quadroon, thought she was about eighty years old. She confessed her name used to be Agatha May Wilson, but that she had changed it upon the advice of Madame Jean when she decided to become "a hoodoo woman." Huddled in her chair before the low fire in the grate, her faint mustache wet and glistening, her eyes bright, she seemed to have no objection to discussing her profession. However, Mrs. Lombardo, the white woman who shared her house and business, kept glancing at her, as if to warn her.

"You can't pay to go to a Voodoo meeting," said Mrs. Lombardo stiffly. "You gotta be invited. That's why lots of people don't believe they still have 'em." A woman of about fifty, very tall and thin, Mrs. Lombardo had black eyes that looked as if their owner was about to lose her temper.

"The sonofabitch is speaking the Lord's truth," said

Madame, who has always been proud of her proficiency at swearing.

"You know we have to be careful," said Mrs. Lombardo. "People misunderstand us." She sighed heavily. "And it is absolutely necessary that you be opened before you can do any work. The opening is really what makes you one of us, but we can't take in nobody unless we can trust 'em."

Madame Cazaunoux had started on the third drink. "Ah, Madame Jean," she cried. "I sure love you, *ma chérie!*"

"Me, I always say the fewer the better," said Mrs. Lombardo. "God knows there's enough of us doing the work now. Of course it is really up to Grandma. She's the one who has the *power*."

Madame put down her glass and tittered. "Goddam!" she said. "Listen who's talking! Some day she's gonna double-cross me. I been warned lots of times. I done taught her too much."

"Shame on you, Grandma," said Mrs. Lombardo. "If you think it's all right I'll go get Rooster." With that she vanished through a door leading into the rear of the house.

As soon as she was gone Grandma shut her eyes and went to sleep. The small room was hot and very odorous. Doors and windows seemed to be sealed, and it was certain that no air had entered the place for weeks. In one corner a shabby iron bed was covered with torn and dirty blankets. Numerous straight-backed chairs lined all the other walls, except in one place near the door leading into the street which was occupied by a small altar covered with white cloth and holding two green candles, one blue and one pink candle, a dried lemon, a rosary and a picture of Saint Peter.

Madame overheard a discussion about the candles. She opened her eyes and looked about the room as if she had never seen the room before. Then she said, "The green candles is for money. They is for Saint Raymond and he is good for money. The pink one is for love, and that is to Saint Anthony. Blue is for Saint Peter. He is good for anything."

Mrs. Lombardo came into the room, followed by a tall colored man who carried a market basket with a white cloth covering it. "Grandma, I brought Rooster," she said. But Grandma was asleep again. From then on she paid little attention to the opening ceremony.

"You-all must do everything Rooster does," said Mrs. Lombardo. "That's the only way this will work."

Rooster began by stripping himself of his coat, vest, tie and shoes. Everyone did the same. Then he spread the tablecloth on the floor in the center of the room.

"Nothing must be crossed," said Mrs. Lombardo. "Be sure your legs and arms ain't crossed or this won't do no good at all and the spirits won't come near us."

Rooster took the picture of Saint Peter from the altar and stood it in the middle of the cloth. Then he began spreading out the articles he had brought concealed in his basket, working silently and quickly, as if it were all routine.

Green and white candles were stood on end on the cloth and other candles of various colors were placed beside these, in a circle around the picture. On each side of this circle he placed a quart bottle, one containing cider, the other raspberry pop. He laid saucers and small dishes here and there, one filled with steel dust on the right side of the picture, another holding dried orris root in front of it. A plate of dried basile was placed on the other side of the picture and another plate, containing the flat hard cakes called "stage planks," was put in front of the dried basile. Behind the picture he laid a five-cent box of gingersnaps. Around the edges of the cloth he laid dishes containing mixed birdseed, cloves and cinnamon, and on each side a bowl of *congris*. A small bottle of olive oil was placed at the very far edge of the cloth

on the left side, and behind this was placed a small paper
sack of sugar. On the far right he put a hand of bananas with
a saucer of small red apples nestling close to it. A branch
from a camphor tree was carefully laid in front of the picture. Then, in front of all, he placed a pint of gin and a
bottle of beer.

Rooster now took a box of matches from his pocket and
lighted the candles. Mrs. Lombardo turned off the single
electric bulb that dangled from a cord in the middle of the
room. The room suddenly became alive with light and shadow,
and the face of the Voodoo man seemed to come to life with
it. Until now he had seemed a sullen, dull-witted being,
performing some meaningless and mechanical motions, but
now his thin face was tense, his eyes glittered and his lips
were drawn back, showing pointed animal-teeth.

Rooster knelt on one knee and everyone did the same.
He rapped on the floor three times and said the Lord's Prayer
in Creole, and everyone again followed suit.

This over, he sprang quickly to his feet and began a song,
at the same time turning in circles, first slowly then more
rapidly. All the participants imitated him. He flung his arms
over his head, glared fiercely toward the ceiling and chanted
his song louder and louder until it seemed he must be heard
a block away. He stopped this as suddenly as he had started
and stood quivering and shaking, his eyes shut now, his arms
straight out before him, his fists clenched and trembling. He
seemed to be in a trance. He came out of this with a loud
grunt, his lids raised and his lips moved. Sounds poured forth
in a coarse guttural outburst that no one could understand.
"The spirits is on him," said Mrs. Lombardo, in a shrill whis-
per. "He is speaking in the unknown tongue."

He stopped and picked up the bottle of gin, removed the
cap, placed the bottle to his lips and took a deep swallow. A
third of the contents of the bottle vanished. Still holding the

flask in one hand, he began to whirl again, singing the same song and stopping to take additional, though smaller, drinks. Now he began another kind of dance, a sort of cakewalk, with intricate forward and backward steps, until he was standing in front of Mrs. Lombardo, who had also been executing the same sort of dance. Stopping before her, he took a mouthful of the gin and spat it directly into her face. She fell back, shuddering and with both hands over her eyes. "We got it now!" she screamed. "We got it! We got it! We got it!"

Rooster sprang at her, swung her from the floor and over his back and began whirling with her in this position. She shrieked in ecstasy, her arms spread out, her legs flailing the air. When he set her down, she fell to her knees and remained there, her eyes shut, low gasps emanating from her lips, long shudders vibrating through her body. Each person in the room except Grandma, who still slept peacefully, was given a whirl on Rooster's back and each ended on his knees before the altar.

Now Rooster dragged a tub from one corner of the room and into this tin vessel he poured the contents of the bottle of beer, the bottle of cider and the one of raspberry pop. Then he added a little of everything in the saucers and plates on the altar. In this mixture he washed the feet of each of the participants, this rite being conducted in silence, except for soft sucking noises Rooster kept making from between his pointed teeth. The insides of everyone's shoes were then rubbed with a mixture of steel dust, dried basile and cinnamon, so, as Mrs. Lombardo explained, "good luck will always guide your feet."

Each person was given a small white candle also for good luck and a green one to guarantee that he would always have money. As he gave out the candles, Rooster passed the flame of each through his mouth to extinguish it. He took a red candle and broke it into small pieces and distributed these pieces. This was for evil work, though of what sort he didn't explain, other than that each piece could be lighted and burned while the owner concentrated upon someone he disliked.

The apples and cakes were also given away. The apples were to be thrown into the path of a person smaller than one's self, thus giving one power over that person. The cakes were to be given to the birds. "They is the dove," said Rooster, "and the dove is the Lord." He then offered to sell the water in which the feet had been bathed for a dollar a pint. "It's good to wash your front steps with to keep enemies out," he carefully explained. There were no sales.

Madame Cazaunoux woke with a grunt. "Me, I was the best damn hoodoo queen what ever lived!" she exclaimed, apparently for no reason at all, except that she seemed to be in the best of moods. "Outside of Marie Laveau I was the best. You hear me, Mimmie, I was the best."

"Grandma, you're sure a case," said Mrs. Lombardo.

"You goddam fools, I was the best," said the old woman, grinning broadly.

It was over, and it was a relief to step out into the brisk winter night. This had been a Voodoo rite and everyone present was now technically a Voodoo. Yet in a few minutes it all seemed unreal and very far away. A huge plane climbed past the stars overhead. This was 1944. This was a period we fancied was modern and fairly free from superstition. A century ago Voodoo might have been a living thing, but the last Marie Laveau had been dead for more than forty years.

"How many people in New Orleans believe in Voodoo?" someone had asked Mrs. Lombardo.

"Plenty," she said. "I don't know exactly how many, of course, but there are a lot of hoodoo churches and things like that. Of course it ain't only in New Orleans. It's all over the country. But I guess there are more workers here than anywhere else. In this town there must be thousands of people that follow it."

"Thousands?"

"Sure," she said. "It ain't all alike. They have different kinds like everything else. Then there are lots of people who say they don't believe in it that are sure scared of it. I seen some funny things."

# 19
# The Saint from Chicago

FROM the beginning of the twentieth century small notes in the newspapers of New Orleans testified to the fact that Voodoo was still a living force.

The arrival of Doctor Koku was announced in 1902. Doctor Koku claimed to have come from the Congo and boasted of having discovered the Seal of Solomon on the shores of Syria. He rented a small cottage a few blocks from where the Laveaus had lived, and opened up for business. When the newspapers refused to take seriously his claim of possession of supernatural powers, he called at their offices and protested. He said he would be in the city but a short time, that he was en route to visit the Grand Lama of Tibet and that he had $42,000,000 in cash. His practices had a pseudo-Oriental flavor, but were fundamentally the same as those of all the Voodooiennes in the city. No one seems to have paid much attention to him, and he vanished without further publicity.

During the same year Henry Duplantier was accused of persecuting a Mrs. Collins by letting her know that he had placed a Voodoo curse upon her. She brought him into court and he was fined.

In 1906 a group of Voodoos asked the police to arrest their leader, Pastor J. V. Larson, on a charge of embezzling the funds of the sect. Pastor Larson headed an organization known, frankly, as the "Voodoo Church."

Charles Baker was arrested in 1913. He was charging property owners fifty cents each for five-cent candles. He claimed that if the candles were burned in vacant houses tenants would appear to rent them.

Numa Luabre was accused of killing cats with his bare hands in 1915, this act accompanying other weird rites. Indignant neighbors testified that Numa caused them all sorts of bad luck. One woman said it was his fault that she remained childless.

During World War I the newspapers were, as during the Civil War, too concerned with other issues to give much space or thought to Voodoo. However, afterward, and until the present time, the small paragraphs telling of curses and charms, even of Voodoo killings—and these sometimes cause much excitement—continue to appear.

Internes and nurses at Charity Hospital are very conscious of the existence of Voodoo. For many years they have been treating patients who insist they have been "hoodooed." Many bring their *gris-gris* to the hospital with them and keep it with them when they are put to bed. The New Orleans *Item*, April 13, 1924, told how hospital attendants found ". . . metal pieces shaped like devils' souls; metal pieces with 'luck signs' upon them; plain metal pieces, coins, colored and knotted strings; straps with fish scales; obas or bags filled with mystic stones and teeth; bones and mosquito bar rings." The article stated that these and many other things were found upon patients at the hospital and that ". . . they will fight and cry to keep them. And there is a story that one man died after his charm was taken from him. The Voodoo doctors, or charm makers, are scattered all over the city. One, a rather famous one, is found on Tuesdays, in Jefferson Market. When one wishes to employ his *power*, one goes to the market and walks up and down three times. When the 'old man who knows' walks away, the client follows."

Despite constant rumors that they still exist, it is extremely doubtful that any celebrations near the Bayou St. John or Lake Pontchartrain ever took place after the Malvina Latour period. Since then all the ceremonies seem to have been conducted indoors, in the homes of practitioners or in churches or temples bearing names designed to conceal their true character. And more emphasis seems to have been placed on the use of *gris-gris*, the placing and removing of curses, and of the practice of homeopathic magic than on the dances and orgies once so commonplace. Yet there are still authentic accounts of rites taking place that are not far removed from those of earlier years. In *Fabulous New Orleans* Lyle Saxon tells of attending one that would have done credit to either of the Laveaus, this sometime around 1926. However, these are, though they may occur more frequently than is imagined, comparatively rare, while cases of people being "hoodooed" are constantly brought to public notice.

One of the most commonplace scenes of the working of the *power* is a graveyard. Not only are voodoo "plants" of various sorts found before the many burial places supposed to contain the remains of the Marie Laveaus, but many other tombs and graves are used to put *gris-gris* on certain individuals.

St. Roch Cemetery in lower New Orleans, a very old place of burial, has seen much of Voodoo. In March, 1931, two women went to place flowers upon the grave of their mother, who had died fifteen years before. As they were about to place their flowers in the vase before the plot they noticed a stump of a black candle almost concealed in a small mound of freshly turned earth in the center of the grave. Their curiosity aroused, they dug into the ground beneath the candle and brought forth an old tobacco can that was sealed tightly and bound with string. When they opened this they found inside a photograph of a man unknown to them, a package of needles and some charred scraps of paper. The picture of the man was also charred around the edges.

The women went to the police, protesting that while they were not afraid of Voodoo they did not like the idea of this defiling of their mother's grave.

"Who is the man marked for Voodoo vengeance?" wrote a reporter in *The Morning Tribune* of the next day. "Were the needles part of a *gris-gris* put on him by some dark magic? Put there so that, according to the Voodoo faith, he would die when his picture crumbled to dust? Was the black candle burning a dire death vigil of the Styx? The picture was charred about the edges and punctured with numerous needle holes symbolic, in Voodooism, of the fate to be visited on the man pictured."

The mystery was never solved, the identity of the young man was never discovered, and no one ever knew whether the curse was thwarted by the discovery of the tobacco can before the picture rotted or whether, despite this, the victim met his doom.

In 1937 an even more elaborate "plant" was found in the same cemetery. The sexton was walking along one of the aisles one morning when he discovered it before a tomb. The earth had been scraped away, leaving a cleared, circular place, around which a ring of candles had been placed. Crosses and other symbols marked the ground. In the very center of the circle reposed an ox tongue, split down the center and sewed back into one piece with black cotton thread. The tongue was opened and inside were three nickels, some red peppers, some pins and several scraps of white paper containing undecipherable writing in black pencil. The police recalled an almost identical "plant" that had been found several years before in front of a tomb in St. Louis Cemetery No. 1. On this occasion one of the pieces of paper contained the name of the current police superintendent. Then it was said that "some Negro who has landed in jail has gotten a Voodoo doctor to wish something on the police." The latest ox tongue case also went unsolved. The family owning the tomb before which this "plant" was found knew nothing of either Voodoo or any enemy who might believe in it.

The sexton at St. Roch Cemetery vowed recently that he

keeps an anxious eye ready for any signs of Voodoo mischief. Nevertheless, he still finds evidence of such abuse of his graveyard.

"The stupidest and cruelest thing I ever seen," he said angrily, "was when we found the dressed-up chicken. You know it's mean as hell to leave food and water near a poor livin' creature and then tie up its feet so it can't reach it. The sonsofbitches who done that better not let me ever catch 'em. The chicken we found was a big rooster and it was all dressed up in a coat and pants, a hat, a collar and a tie. His legs was tied wit' about a hundred yards of white cord. On the tomb where he was I found three nickels. I took that rooster home, but the poor thing died.

"A few days after that a colored woman I know come in here and I asked her what all this monkeyshine meant. She said it was hoodoo. Somebody was in jail and he ain't the right one to be there, so his friends took a rooster, dressed it like a man and tied it up in the cemetery so it would suffer. As long as that rooster suffered the guilty man was supposed to suffer and in the end he was supposed to confess and give himself up. Them people are crazy.

"I've found plenty of stuff in this place, mostly in the back, in the Negro section. I've caught people buryin' tongues all stuck wit' needles and pins and wrapped around wit' black thread. I found a lemon split and sprinkled wit' red and black pepper and wit' a note in it that had a man's name written nine times. Once I found a pair of tan shoes wit' a note between the sole and heel that said, 'Willie, I want your death.' Another time we found three pigs' hearts, all tied together, and less than ten minutes later one of my helpers came across a loaf of bread and some fried pork chops. We'd have thought it was somebody's lunch if each of them pork chops hadn't had nine pins stickin' up in it."

This sexton knew a Voodoo doctor who had tried to use

St. Roch's Cemetery for Voodoo purposes for a long time.

"This man's name was Hunter," said the irate guardian of the graves. "He was a big cream-colored guy that never did a day's honest work in his life, but always had plenty money. He lived near here and all day and half the night women was comin' in and out his house—white and black. Sometimes the white women come in automobiles and dressed like they had money.

"Hunter used to come here and ask me to sell him some grease from the bell in the chapel, and I'd do it. He said he used it to cure people of sores. It was real funny. When I couldn't get any grease from the bell I used to swipe it from automobiles that was parked outside the graveyard. He didn't know the difference and he used to always brag how many people he cured wit' that chapel bell grease. That always tickled me.

"It went on for a long time, but then he started messin' around in the place too much, digging up dirt and taking dust from the tops of tombs to sell as goofer dust. People don't like all that goin' on in here, and I began to get complaints. Well, one time he come in here wit' a big blonde woman and I heard 'em talkin'. Everything he'd say she'd giggle and scream, 'Oh, Doctor! Really? You sure are smart!' and stuff like that. I didn't like that. You can't have that goin' on if you tryin' to keep a place respectable. So the next time he come I put him out. I told him I was gonna get the police after him if he step inside this place again.

"I never did bother wit' any hoodoo doctors after that. I don't see why they come here. Why pick on me? Hell, this town is lousy wit' graveyards!"

During the early decades of the present century many other kinds of sorcery and pseudo-science either lent to or borrowed from Voodoo superstitions and practices. Many fortune tellers, palmists, healers and spiritualists added to their repertoires the dark magic that had been African. Marie Laveau I and Marie II had told fortunes and had talked of communication with the spirit world, but now it was the other way around and Voodoo began to be popular with all types of soothsayers and magicians.

After World War I there was the great vogue of spiritualism that swept from England to America, as a blood-drenched world grieved for its dead youth and yearned to communicate with those sacrificed in the carnage. Séances became popular, and every town had its mediums who entertained groups with table rappings and ectoplasmic manifestations. At home people played with ouija boards and automatic writing. For some it was a serious and pathetic effort to reach into the other world. For others it was a game and a fad.

Voodoos had long talked of spirits, but this referred to demons and personifications of evil, not the departed dead. However in 1921 Mother Leafy Anderson arrived in New Orleans and with her, though unseen by ordinary eyes, stalked the spirit of an Indian chief, Black Hawk, who was destined to become a Voodoo saint, for Mother Anderson was a missionary and, as she said later, when she opened her church, she "had a message for the people."

A middle-aged colored woman who operated several spiritualist churches in Chicago, Mother Anderson was not a Voodoo. There was a great deal of Voodoo in Chicago as there was—and is—in all American cities with large Negro populations. Pupils of the two Laveaus had spread the beliefs and practices throughout the country. But Leafy Anderson claimed to detest Voodoo and to be its enemy.

Mother Anderson was the founder of many spiritualist churches that are now so popular in New Orleans among colored people and a poorer class of whites. Immediately upon her arrival in the city she opened a church and also a class to train women who wished to become "Mothers" and to follow her teachings.

Mother Doris, who now has her own church, was trained by Mother Anderson and remembered that "there was eighty-five to one hundred of us in her first class and she charged a dollar a lesson. She taught healin' and prophesyin' and callin' up spirits. Of course most of 'em didn't ever finish 'cause everybody ain't got the *power*, but most of the Mothers in New Orleans now learned what they know from Mother Anderson." Mother Doris described how Mother Anderson dressed for her services. "Sometimes she wore all white wit' a purple veil, but other times she wore a gold gown wit' a Black Hawk mantle over her shoulders; it had a picture of Black Hawk sewed on it. Once in a while she wore a man's full dress suit, but that was only for special occasions."

All present day "Mothers" deny they practice Voodoo, and many of them don't. However, others use many of the oils and powders and sell a mild sort of *gris-gris*. Orleanians are quite accustomed to seeing the "Mothers" in the streets, for almost all of them wear their robes and headdresses at all times, but strangers are startled at the sight of the women in their trailing gowns of white, or gold brocade, or blue velvet, with matching veils that hang to the middle of their backs. There are two white "Mothers" in the city, both of whom were trained by Mother Anderson, and who both operate churches with large congregations composed of both races. Mother Anderson died in 1927, but she still appears to the women who carry on her work and gives instructions as to her wishes.

"Black Hawk is the saint for the South," said Mother Edwards, a huge fat Negress, who always wears a gown and veil of deep red satin. "Mother Anderson told us there was another Indian saint named White Hawk that took care of the North. We don't know much about him, but any time you wants to chase away evil you call Black Hawk and he'll take care of you."

Nearly all these spiritualist churches have statues of Black Hawk among the images of bona fide saints, for the churches are odd conglomerations of many sects. Most of them exhibit Roman Catholic statues and candles, and use incense and holy water. They sing Baptist and Methodist hymns, and the congregation "testifies" and suffers attacks of the "jumps" and the "jerks," such as are common to all cults of the revivalist type. The "Mothers" heal by prayer and the laying on of hands, hold spiritualist séances, and sometimes tell fortunes as a side line. And, though they all deny it, they sometimes do business in *gris-gris*. Their sincerity varies. Some are, apparently, extremely sincere and are known to do a great deal of charitable work among the poor of their neighborhoods. Others are outright charlatans and have accumulated small fortunes by duping the ignorant.

But, whether he likes it or not, Black Hawk has been adopted by the real Voodoos. Madame Cazaunoux thought very highly of him.

"He's new and he's young," said the old woman, "and, me, I didn't pay him no mind for a long time, but, goddamit, you gotta admit he's sure good when you is in trouble. I tried him lots of times and he sure has got a lot of *power*."

# 20
# Lala

IF there is a living successor to the Voodoo throne it is probably Lala. Her reputation had preceded her.

"Lala is a devil. She wears a shawl over her head to hide her horns," said a colored woman who lives near her. "If I sees her comin' I crosses the street or goes 'round the block to keep from meetin' her. There ain't no tellin' what she will do."

But the first thing Lala said about herself was "I don't do no more bad work. I used to do plenty, I gotta admit, and I still knows how to do it, but I has changed. I has even changed in my looks. I used to be a big woman, but I been messin' wit' the spirits too long. They got me down."

Like all present day Voodooiennes Lala has mingled spiritualism with Voodoo. Physically, she is a poor substitute for the exotic Laveaus. Small, so thin her dark brown skin seems to cling to her bones, with prominent eyes and high cheekbones, Lala is sinister only when she laughs. Then something happens. She flings her head back, closes her eyes, opens a mouth filled with jagged yellow teeth and emits a shrill screech that is bloodcurdling. She is very untidy, long grayish underwear always showing below the sleeves of the dirty brown dress she almost always wears, her naked feet thrust into man's shoes, a plaid shawl drawn over her head and pinned beneath her chin with a rusty safety pin. But when the shawl comes off there are no horns.

Her house consists of two rooms, and is inhabited by Lala, her husband Louie, and her sister Adeline. The front room is always crowded with furniture, including a large china closet filled with cheap china and glassware, a sideboard piled with vases, dishes, clothes and old newspapers, a double bed, an upright piano and at least a half dozen chairs. The walls are hung with religious pictures and near the door leading into the other room is a small altar holding candles and a picture, cut from a newspaper and framed, that Lala says is of Marie Laveau. Investigation proved it to be an imaginative pen-and-ink drawing that had accompanied an article on Voodoo published some years ago.

"I ain't as good as she was," Lala confessed. "She was a crack. But I can do lots of things. If the chickens had laid an egg today I could make it walk for you. You know what I done already? I stopped the rope. There was a man gonna be hanged like next week, unless the judge changed his mind. I got me a piece of ice and went to the courthouse and put it under the judge's chair. When that hunk of ice melted the old judge's heart melted, too, and the man was saved. I is good! You ask them niggers on Orleans Street 'bout somethin' else I done. There was a woman over there what had a great big belly. Somebody had done fed her snail powder in cabbage. I give her silver powder, made from real silver, and I got twenty-nine snails and three frogs out of her. After that she never had no more trouble at all."

Lala punctuated her conversation with the living in the room by making occasional remarks to the many spirits who she says surround her constantly. At times she walked back and forth from the street entrance to the door leading to the back room, spitting on the floor. "Know what I'm doin'?" was the explanation. "I'm payin' off. You hear me, Miss Kelly? I'm payin' off!"

"Miss Kelly give me my piano," she said. "You know that piano done already played by itself? I was in bed one night and I heared the strings. I say, 'That you, Miss Kelly? Come on in here. I ain't scared of you.' But them strings just kept on playin' a tune Miss Kelly used to always like. I knowed right then she wanted me to do somethin' for her. I didn't wait at all. I got out my bed and went straight to the graveyard and put some *congris* under one of her flowerpots. When I went back the next week all that *congris* was done gone."

Lala held her meeting in the second room, which was more crowded than the first, holding, besides a rickety kitchen stove, a bed, a large table, a trunk and numerous chairs, four dogs, three cats, a parrot in a cage and a pet goose that waddled about as if it owned the establishment. In the yard beyond the back door were chickens, ducks and some pigeons. "I ain't got no more snake," Lala said, apologetically. "You really ought to have one to do hoodoo work, but them mean niggers around here reported me and the policemens come and make me give it to the zoo up at Audubon Park. It sure make me mad. If I still did bad work I would fix 'em. How I gonna work at all wit'out no snake?"

A man entered from the back yard and this proved to be Lala's husband, a quiet, rather docile Negro, who was very cordial and polite. "I had signed Louie up for life," Lala said. "I puts him out all the time and he always comes back. Ain't that so, Louie?"

Louie nodded meekly. Apparently he feared Lala and she was the dominating one of the two. At her direction, he cleaned off the table in the center of the room and instructed everyone present to sit in a certain place at the table. In the middle she placed two white candles and lighted them. Standing at one end, she extended her arms and said, "Now watch me how I does this."

Her finger tips just above the flames, she said, "C'mon, rise up! Do what I says." The flames obeyed and rose higher. "Now make five points!" she ordered dramatically. Each flame, though somewhat reluctantly, it seemed, divided itself into exactly five points. Lala took a seat at the head of the table, grinning proudly.

"Now I'll show you something else," she said. "Louie, bring me an egg." She had forgotten her former excuse.

The egg was produced and she placed it in a small jelly glass in an upright position so that one end of the egg rose a fraction of an inch above the rim of the glass. On top of the egg she placed a broom straw in a position pointing away from herself. "Now point to me," she said to the straw. It failed to move. "I knowed it," she said. "That woman next door is snappin' her fingers to keep the spirits away from me. Marie Laveau, help me, darlin'. You knows I is your friend.

"I've had plenty trouble," Lala admitted. "I been pulled in lots of times, but they can't do me nothin'. One time I told a judge to give me his ring and I'd make it walk. When he seen his ring walkin' away he said, 'You is sure a smart woman.' Then he let me go. You see, I been studyin' all my life. I read all them hoodoo books, *Tit Albert* and *Black Hawk* and lots of others. The doctor say I got a abscess on my brain and I knows that's what caused it. *Black Hawk* is about that Indian spirit, you know, and that's the worst of 'em. It's got white writin' on black paper and it sure is dangerous.

"I tell you what I can do: I can make a person droopy and sleepy by hullin' out a red apple like a cup and puttin' the person's name inside written on a piece of paper. Then I fills it up wit' the stuff I took out the apple and hangs it up in my chimney on a wire. When the smoke reach it the person just can't keep their eyes open, and soon they go to bed and start sleepin'. If I keep the apple there long enough they gonna die.

"If you want to make a man stay wit' a woman one way is to take and light three candles and put 'em on a table. Stick your arm wit' a pin until you draw blood. Mix your blood wit' black ink and write the man's name nine times on a sheet of paper. Promise if it work you gonna pay off to Onzoncaire—he's a powerful hoodoo spirit and he can do anything for you. That's what I done to Louie. He can't never leave me now. But don't forget to pay off. You gets a sheep's head and pours a bottle of whiskey down its mouth. At twelve o'clock take this out on a country road and wear a red night-gown and a red cap on your head, and your bare feets. Put the sheep's head under a oak tree and say, 'Onzoncaire, that's for you.' Then walk home backward. One thing you got to watch is not to walk on no *banquette*. Always keep in the middle of the road or the street.

"I done a lot for the women in the sportin' houses. I made 'em put red powder on one leg and green powder on the other. They got so many men they couldn't handle the business.

"To make people go away you melt a black candle and knead the wax like dough. Write the person's name on a piece of paper four times frontward and five times backward. Roll your wax into a ball and put this paper in the middle of it. Then stick nine pins in the ball. Get on the ferry and go out to the middle of the river and throw it in. Snap your fingers and say, 'St. Expédite, make him go quick!' You know St. Expédite is the saint who gets things done in a hurry and he's awful good for hoodoo work. Has you ever heared people say, 'I'm on needles and pins today'? Well, that's the ball workin'. When they goes away take a piece of poundcake and go to Our Lady of Guadalupe Church on North Rampart Street and leave it in front of his statue. Another way to get rid of somebody is to make a stuffed man or woman and put it in a little boat you buy at the ten-cent store. You floats this in the river and asks St. Expédite to help you. When the boat gets to the ocean the person's gonna go away."

Lala turned her head. "You make some coffee, Louie. Me, I always likes some coffee when I'm talkin' 'bout my work."

While Louie dripped the coffee Lala decided to do a Voo-doo dance. "I knows all them real hoodoo dances," she said. She puts her hands on her hips and did a shuffling dance which consisted mostly of stepping forward twice, then backward once, some shaking of her bony hips and shoulders, and much rolling of her prominent eyes.

"When Marie Laveau danced she held a big fish up high and she shaked all over," Lala said. "Like this!" She lifted her arms and held an imaginary fish, and her body moved faster with shoulders, hips and eyes rolling in unison. "That is a real hoodoo dance," she said. "Nobody but me knows how to do it now."

Louie brought the coffee and she tilted her cup and spilled a few drops on the floor. "That for you, Marie Laveau," she said.

"I can run a person crazy," she boasted. "I take the bark off a tree and get me a guinea hen egg. I writes the person's name around the guinea egg nine times and stick it in the hole of the tree I took the bark from. Then I puts back the bark and I makes nine crosses on the outside. After that I pray to that tree once a week for five months. When the person go crazy I gives Tit Albert a soup plate. He's the hoodoo saint that loves soup plates. I buries it under the tree. I used to get paid five hundred dollars for that work.

"If somebody is already crazy and they wants to get back their good sense, I takes a white dove and splits it in half. I sits the crazy man in a chair and puts the two halves of the dove on top his head and holds 'em there until all the blood run down his face. After all the blood run out I wash his face in a white bowl and throw the bowl in the river wit' three nickels. That costs $500, too."

Her coffee finished and Louis vanished into the front room, she decided to perform a little ceremony.

"Everybody get down on their knees," she said. She knelt and closed her eyes. "Stars above, saints, everybody, help us to get what we wants," she prayed. "Spirits, give us the *power* to do all the good work we want to do and the *power* to do bad work when we gotta do it. Spirits, hear us and help us!"

She rapped three times on the floor with her right fist. "Spirits," she said, "if you hears us, let there be smoke!" It was a startling fact that at that moment both candles on the table began to smoke.

This excited Lala. "We has the spirits now," she said. "All right, you people has the spirits your way. You is all gonna be big hoodoo people. I can see that." She rose, said, "I'll be back in a minute," and disappeared into the other room.

When she reappeared she was in costume. And what a costume! The skirt had ruffles of every color in the rainbow and some violent enough to dim any rainbow. She wore an equally elaborate blouse and an unidentifiable headdress that had an orange fringe. Behind her came Louie, wearing a red and green costume and carrying two guitars, one of which he handed to Lala.

"We was gypsies last year," she said. "We gonna do a hoodoo dance for you out in the back yard. Louie can play and I'll dance."

Lala chased chickens and ducks away from a spot near the fence that separated her yard from the one next door and instructed Louie to "get the stuff." He brought a china plate, some pink candles, a milk bottle filled with bay rum and an empty pint bottle that had contained gin. The plate was placed on the ground, the candles were stood in the plate and lighted. While Louie sat on a box and strummed on his guitar Lala hopped and danced around the plate, frequently raising one leg and passing it over the candles, then doing the same thing with the other. After she tired she played while Louie danced. Louie hopped like a frog, the gin pint in one hand, the bottle of bay rum in the other. He kept throwing his head back so violently that each time his neck cracked audibly.

Once you gain Lala's confidence she is generous with her secrets, but she does not trust many people. She moves her residence at least three times a year because too many people

come to ask her questions. All Negroes of the poorer class
in New Orleans know of her existence. Most of them agree
that she knows more about "hoodoo" than anyone else. Lala
credits her knowledge to a Madame Touro. "Madame Touro
trained me," she said. "And she was trained by Marie Laveau.
That is why I is so good." She knows of only one Marie
Laveau, probably Marie II.

Her reputation for being evil persists. "That Lala is the
worst creature in the world," said a maid in a large office building in the business section of the city. "She will do any bad
thing you can think of. Stay away from Lala. She's dangerous and she's bad."

Of herself, Lala said, "I ain't troublin' nobody if they treat
me right, but I can sure go to my end if they do me a trick.
It's evil for evil with me. One of my cats got poisoned and
died and I knowed the man what done it. I burned a black
candle on him and now he's got bronchitis and the doctors
done gave up hope on him. Now I don't really do no more
bad work, but if people does stuff to you what you does back
ain't bad. They got it comin' to 'em. That's the truth."

Lala does possess an apparently endless store of Voodoo
knowledge.

"To protect yourself against bein' crossed," she said, "get
some garlic, sage, thyme, geranium water, dry basile, parsley
and five cents of saltpeter. You bathe in this on Monday,
Wednesday and Friday. Rub your body good with bay rum
when you get through, then with verbena essence and jack
honeysuckle. Ain't nobody can hurt you then. You is uncrossed and you is gonna stay uncrossed.

"If you want to win a court case put the witnesses' names
in a beef tongue and tie the tongue and fold it over. That
will keep 'em from speakin'. Take Black Candle tobacco and
salt and put it on ice and burn a black candle in front of it.
If you wants to keep the judge and the district attorney from

sentencin' the person you puts their names in a mixture of nine lumps of sugar, honey, a little strawberry syrup and some Follow-Me-Boy Oil. Mix all this in a plate and light a yellow candle in the middle of it. Then ask the old folks— that's what I calls the spirits sometimes; they is older than us, ain't they?—to help you.

"To make a runaway girl come home all you got to do is burn her clothes in a pan of gasoline wit' some chicken droppin's. To keep your boss from firin' you, write his name on a piece of paper and bury it in your yard wit' a chopped up red candle and a black cat's tail.

"I know an easy *gris-gris* to send a person straight to the dogs," Lala continued. "You just gotta give him some boiled rat soup to drink. Mix up some vegetables and everything just like a real soup and cook a rat in it. It won't taste bad or nothin', but when that soup gets to workin' on the person he is gonna act like he's crazy and is gonna go straight down to the dogs.

"A good thing is to make cats call spirits. This ain't hard, but you gotta be careful. Kill a black cat in a graveyard at twelve o'clock sharp and take out his guts. Cook the guts in plenty hot lard mixed wit' salt and raw eggs and eat 'em as soon as they is lukewarm. After that you go back to the graveyard the next Friday night and call that cat. When he starts answerin' you call out names of dead people you knows. Ask anything you want about 'em. Tell the cat you believes in the devil. The best month for this is October; then you is sure to see a spirit when the cat answer your call. And if you ever sees a spirit once you can see 'em all the time. They will talk to you just like human bein's.

"If you wants real *power*, real evil *power*, keep after that cat until you gets to talk to the devil himself. When he come you tell him you wants to denounce the world and wants to control his evil spirits. You gotta say you will give up everything for him. Pray to him for six nights so he can be sure you is on his side. Pray to Marie Laveau. She'll help you. Ask the devil to summon her from her throne in Hell and then get her to help you. But let me tell you something: you is gotta keep every promise you make to the devil. He sure will get you if you ever goes back on him. I seen it happen. When he takes you into his service he puts a mark over your bed. From then on you is his, and you can control spirits. You is been blessed by the devil and you is one of his agents on earth."

At this point Lala crossed herself. Asked why, she replied, "I ain't never sold myself to the devil yet. As I told you I don't hardly ever do no bad work. I used to be terrible. I used to take a turtle and eat his heart while he was still alive. That keeps you from harm, for true. I used to boil goat's milk and parsley and grate a silver dime in it and drink that. That is sure good. It really cleans you out, and nobody can hoodoo you wit' anything.

"I can make a man and woman fight by takin' a dirt dauber, cayenne pepper, filé, flaxseed, graveyard dirt and gunpowder and throwin' it against their house. That makes hell in the camp! Then I throw War Powder against the side of the house. That brings a patrol ride.

"To make a marriage you take Saint Joseph's picture and put sand in front of it, write the couple's names in the sand and stand candles around in a circle. Then get a boy doll and a girl doll, tie their hands together wit' a white satin ribbon and put them in the middle. Then pray to Saint Joseph to make this marriage for you. When he make it, pay off by puttin' macaroni and parsley in the sand. See, I can make 'em and I break 'em. That's the way I is!

"Any time you got a woman who is foolin' wit' another man just get some Black Devil Oil from the drugstore, mix it wit' sugar and salt and sprinkle this all over her clothes, 'specially her underwear. She ain't gonna mess wit' no man but you after that."

While Lala believes in spirits and swears she converses with them every day she does not like the organized spiritualist churches. "That religion is the bunk," she said. "All religions is all right in a way, but I don't like them people. Me, I is really a Catholic. You seen me cross myself, didn't you? I don't like spiritualist meetin's. I goes to a hoodoo meetin' some fishermen holds every Friday night, and that is different. They got a man named Gould there that burns a candle in a skull. He sure is good. He prays to Marie Laveau and he can call up Black Hawk. He helps me wit' my landlords. I ain't never been put out of no house for not payin' my rent, I'll tell you that."

Lala seemed tired of talking now. She stood up and began to quiver and shake. "The spirits is on me right now," she groaned. "They is right in this room. You all gonna get everything you wants. My *power* is sure workin'. You hear me, Miss Kelly? Darlin', you gonna help me, ain't you? I knows you is always wit' me." She stamped on the floor three times. "That damn woman next door is still snappin' her fingers," she said, "but it ain't gonna harm me. I knows how to stop her from *crossin'* me!"

Asked about Madame Cazaunoux and Mrs. Lombardo, she said, "You gotta watch 'em. Them people is sharp!" Voodooiennes do not trust each other.

# 21
# The Queen of Perdido Street

THE people around Perdido Street are afraid of Julia Jackson. They do not avoid passing her on the street as they do Lala, but they treat her with a great deal of respect and they do not like to talk about her. Julia is more intelligent and has more education than Lala. She is shrewd and calculating and, it is said, very revengeful. Despite all her foolishness and her ignorance there is a bit of the mystic in Lala. Julia Jackson is a business woman.

Very black and over six feet tall, with eyes that are slightly crossed, you can never tell whether Julia is looking at you or at the devil seated on your shoulder, for she says that many persons carry these evil beings on their shoulders all their lives without knowing it.

"As soon as I see a person coming," Julia said, "I know right away if they has signed up with the devil and if they has one of his demons is riding that person's shoulder and grinning happy as can be about it." Julia laughed when she said this, and her eyes looked as if they were seeing demons then.

Perdido Street is a few blocks above Canal Street, and the section of it that is dominated by Julia lies just off South Rampart Street on what Orleanians refer to as the "Lake Side." Inhabited by Negroes of a low financial stratum, the street corners are nearly all occupied by cheap and noisy saloons and the locale reeks of stale beer and sweat and garbage.

During the day things are rather quiet. A few loafers drink in the bars and the women sit on their stoops and gossip.

Sometimes they seem to look up at the sky, almost as if they were impatient for the coming of night.

When darkness comes Perdido Street returns to life. The barrooms turn on their signs, the juke boxes begin to blast out their jazz and swing music, and the places crowd with night creatures—prostitutes, drug addicts and petty criminals among them. There is much drinking of sherry wine, at five cents per glass, and of gin, at ten cents. Police hang on the corners and do not look particularly pleased with their assignment. The women sell themselves, sometimes for fifty cents, sometimes in dark alleys.

But, day or night, when Julia Jackson strides past there is a hush and a silence and many greetings of "Hello, Miss Julia!" "How is you, Miss Julia?" A trifle lame, she nevertheless walks quickly, nodding unsmilingly to those who speak to her. There aren't many who dare ignore her. There is a story that once she killed a man with two strokes of a red pencil on his forehead.

"She's dynamite," said Minnie Lewis, who lived next door to her. "Don't you see how that woman walk? She walk just like Marie Laveau. No, me, I ain't got nothin' to say about her. Some says she does good and some says she does bad. They say everything about her. I done bought a few things from her, but I don't go in much for that stuff."

Julia has been practicing Voodoo for more than thirty years and it has bought her half the property in the block where she lives and an automobile that takes her on trips out into the country, where she has acquired an extensive trade in *gris-gris*. "Country people has more trouble than city people," Julia said. "I got me a good business in the parishes."

The front room of her home contains the usual altar with the candles and pictures of saints and many more bizarre items. "I make all my own stuff," she said. "It saves me money and it's as good. People who has to buy their stuff ain't using their heads."

She doesn't laugh when you tell her how she is feared, but will confess, "They call me lightning and black cloud. They say I walk with the devil in the graveyard at night. But wait until they get in trouble. Who they come to first? Julia Jackson! I don't care what they call me so long as they keep coming and bring me money. I got sense.

"I use all kinds of things in my work," Julia admitted. "Most people like chicken feathers, earthworms, red pepper, coffee grounds, nails, beef tongues, and oils and powders. I done already cured a woman with bay leaf and soda when she was dying of heart trouble. It was partly faith. Don't ever forget the faith part. You gotta believe. But some of the things they say about me ain't true. I don't kill people and never have killed anybody that I know of. Of course hoodoo work is funny work, and sometimes things happen you don't count on.

"I know how to kill people with hoodoo. One way is to catch you a rattlesnake, kill it and hang it in the sun to dry. Write the person's name on a piece of paper and put it in the snake's mouth. Just like that snake dry up the person gonna dry up, too. If you keep that snake in the sun long enough the person's gonna die. That is a true charm.

"Another way to kill is to take a rooster, chop off its head and feets and take them to a graveyard. You can keep the body to cook. When you get to the graveyard put a black candle in the rooster's beak, lay it down in front of a tomb and bury the feets in the ground in the back of the tomb. Light your candle and pray for one hour that this man have bad luck. Then dig up the feets and take them and the head and go bury 'em in the man's yard. He won't last a week.

"The wors' old hoodoo woman I ever knew was Mrs. Crobuzon. She was a old Urai hoodoo what had sold herself to the devil. You know when you do that you gotta kill one of your children every year. She had fifteen children, and she

had already killed twelve when I first knew her. Her husband
died and left her life insurance and she bought a house and
furniture. But she had killed so many of her children that the
spirits of 'em wouldn't let her sleep. I knew a girl named
Lizzie used to always go see her. Lizzie's ma got scared and
made her stop, and you know what Mrs. Crobuzon did? She
put a curse on Lizzie to keep her from getting married, and
the poor girl never did. She did terrible things, that old
woman! Bad as I am, I'd never let her cross my door. She's
broke now and she's only got three children left and they
won't have anything to do with her. She sleep one place
tonight and another tomorrow night, but she can't step over
my sill. She'd like to because I got *power* and I built me a
good business, but I'm not fooling with her.

"I'll tell you something funny I done. A girl came here
and told me she was having trouble with her husband because
he couldn't keep anything he had. When he got paid he lost
his money gambling. When he wasn't gambling he got drunk
and give it away. One time she went out and left him home
and when she came back he'd given away almost all the furniture in the house. He even lost his clothes and his hats. I
listened to her and I gave her some stuff. But about a week
after that she came back and she was weeping and carrying
on like she was out of her mind. 'Miss Julia,' she say, 'what
you done to me? I went home and I rubbed my feet with the
powders and I rubbed his feet with 'em. I put some of your
oil in his food and I sprinkled some on his pillow so he'd
breathe it while he was sleeping. Now you know what happen? I found out all this time he had him another woman and
today he took everything I had and went off with that
woman. Miss Julia, I feel like you double-crossed me. The
way he used to be he'd have forgotten this woman after a
while and he'd have lost her like he done everything else.
Now he done kept her.' I run that girl out of my house fast.
How I know about all that stuff? All I promised her was that

I'd cure her husband of giving everything away. It ain't my fault if it worked. That's what I'm supposed to do—just what people ask. Next day she came back and bought some stuff to make her husband come home. He came all right, but he didn't bring nothing with him. He'd lost everything to that other woman."

Like all Voodoos Julia is afraid to talk at any length about her work. "I know a man is coming after me," she said. "He says my work is illegal, but there ain't a thing illegal if the people want it, is there? If people is willing to pay for something, they ought to have it. It's said that I got rich on this stuff, but I'm not as rich as the politicians what send the police to run me in. How you figure that out?"

She could remember some of the Voodoo celebrations near the turn of the century. "I was just a child," she said, "but my ma was a hoodoo woman and she used to take me to see 'em. The dancers held big Chinese scarfs behind their necks. They would march out to the center of the floor to the beat of tom-toms—and could they dance! You don't see nothing like that nowadays. In those days they could count on the police letting 'em alone as long as they stayed out of town. That's why all the big hoodoo queens held their meetings by Lake Pontchartrain. They was smart women and they knew how to run a first-class business.

"I would have done good in them days," she said. "I do all right now, but I got to be careful. I kind of got the people 'round here bluffed, and there ain't one of them got enough nerve to turn me in. They know what I'm like when I'm mad, and they ain't taking any chances. I have to watch out for the police, though."

John Matthews, who lives around the corner from Julia, thinks she has more *power* than anybody in the world. He swears she made a good woman of his wife, and he had not believed it could be done.

"I had the wors' woman in the world," said John. "I loved her, but she wasn't no good at all. I'd take home my money and she spend it on other men. I was always finding Pullman porters in my bed. I'd beat her and she'd beat me back. We was havin' patrol rides regular every Saturday night. Somebody told me 'bout Miss Julia and I come to see her. Man, the minute I looked at that woman I was scared of her, but I had to do something 'bout my wife.

"Miss Julia took me to her room and I give her five dollars to start wit'. She say she don't never do no work for less than ten dollars, but that was all I had, so she took it. She had all kinds of saints' pictures in her room and I had to walk around and put my hand once on all those pictures. Then she make me swear wit' my hand on a Bible that I was gonna bring her the other five dollars at the end of the week. I swore 'cause I knowed if I tried to fool that woman it was gonna be bad.

" 'Now I'll tell you this,' she said to me. 'I know you is sincere 'cause you was born in April and everybody born in April is sincere. But if you think you can fool me you is crazy. And if you ever tells anybody on me you is gonna pay tenfold for it. Now I'm gonna make your wife sick. She's gonna be so sick you gonna think she is dyin', but she won't die.'

"She give me some white-lookin' stuff and made me kneel down in front of her altar for more 'n an hour. I think I ain't ever gonna get done kneelin'. Then she tell me to put this powder in some mashed potatoes and give 'em to my wife. I was to come back the next Friday and bring my wife's picture.

"Well, I fed my wife that powder all week and ain't nothin' happen. If I hadn't been so scared of Miss Julia I wouldn't have ever gone back to her, but I went and I brought her my wife's picture and the five dollars. Miss Julia made me kneel down in front of her altar again. She put the picture I brought up on the altar and she sprinkled it wit' some red ashes. She kept me kneelin' for a long time and all the time she was jumpin' up and down and shakin' and hollerin' and prayin' and scarin' the hell out of me. After that I went home and fed my old woman some more of that hoodoo powder. Does you know that in three days my wife was layin' up in Charity Hospital wit' doctors all 'round her bed shakin' their heads.

"She sure was sick, and for a long time I thought Miss Julia was wrong and that my wife was gonna die. I still loved her, but I figured she wasn't no good and if she had to live a evil life she might as well die. The doctors all said she had some new kind of disease they ain't never seen before and they all come to look at her and all the time she lay moanin' and groanin' and prayin'—and she never had been no prayin' woman.

"Do you know two weeks later the doctors done changed their minds and told me there ain't nothin' the matter wit' her and I could take her home? And when I brought her home she was like a changed woman. She saved my money for me and she ain't never messed wit' no other men since. I tell you this, I done sent at least ten fellows to Miss Julia to get their womens fixed up, and every time she done the same thing and those womens landed up in Charity Hospital. You can figure any time you see a woman in that place wit' somethin' the matter wit' her that the doctors can't figure out she's got a hoodoo woman workin' on her for that woman's man."

But not all Julia Jackson's clients are Negroes.

Mrs. Armantine Hebert believes she saved her daughter when the girl was suffering under a Voodoo spell.

"Me, I believe in anything that does you good," said Mrs. Hebert. "My daughter was going crazy. No doctor could do nothing for her. Somebody told me about Julia Jackson, and when I went to see her she told me my girl had been hoo-dooed from drinking lemonade. It was for true, because my daughter she had been drinking lots of lemonade to purify her blood. Miss Julia told me to go to my daughter's house and see if I find any powder on her floor and she give me some stuff to wash the powder away and some candles to burn. Me, I go there and sure enough there is powder like roach powder in the corners of the front room. I knew it wasn't roach powder 'cause my daughter is clean like me and she ain't never had a roach to her name. So I washed it all away and burned the candles on the mantelpiece.

"You know right away she started acting like her senses had come back? But it really took Miss Julia six months to cure her. Every week I go and every week she give me different things to help my daughter. The last thing she done was to tell me to comb my daughter's hair and to bring her a little piece of her hair and some ground meat. When I brought those things she made some meat balls and put a piece of my girl's hair inside each one. Me, I kept thinking that was a funny thing to do, yes, but I knew I had to have faith so I didn't say a word. Miss Julia told me to take the meat balls and go for a walk, and every time I see a dog to drop a ball. I done that until they was all gone. I just dropped them and the dogs ate 'em up one by one. I never would look back to see what happened to the dogs, but you know a lady was across the street when I dropped the last meat ball and she tell me the dog that ate it dropped dead? When I got home my daughter was sitting on the gallery making her some curtains—and she ain't done that since she lost her mind. She's fine now and ain't crazy at all.

"Miss Julia can do anything, her! People know it, too. I already seen more automobiles lined up in front of her house than the Roosevelt Hotel is got."

# 22
# Snakes Jumped Out of Her Mouth

FELTIE BUTLER died a hoodoo death. The June night in 1940 that Feltie lay in his gray plush casket, encircled with flowers and "standing" ferns, his family and friends gazed down upon his face and nodded in agreement. Feltie had been *fixed*.

"It jest ain't possible," his wife kept saying. "It jest ain't possible." The doctor had told her that Feltie had succumbed to pneumonia. "Any time a man spits up snails and a frog, he ain't got no pneumonia. Feltie was hoodooed. I don't care what no doctor say!"

According to her, Feltie had been a good man in most ways and had never had an enemy. The only way she could explain what had happened was that some woman had been after him and had become angered when she was spurned. Feltie had a way with women, his wife admitted, saying, "He jest had what it takes, that's all. I never did blame him, 'cause the womens look at him and start hoppin'. You can't blame no man for that." Gazelle Butler seemed proud that her husband had been so attractive to the opposite sex. "That's why I married him," she said. She thought his one fault had been that he liked to drink sherry wine on Saturday nights.

"Feltie worked steady," she said. "Some weeks he made pretty good money. The mens and womens used to be after him all the time, but he never did go no place 'cept on Saturday nights. I always let him go then. I figured a man what stayed home six nights a week ought to go out on the seventh. Ain't every woman got a six-nights husband.

"This Saturday before he died he was feelin' fine. He ate his supper and tol' me he was jest goin' down to the corner to get some scrap iron—that's what he call his sherry, you know. Feltie wasn't a hard drinker, and a man gotta have some fun, so I didn't mind. Couldn't hold him down too much anyway; he was a high-spirited man. But, after he was gone a long time, me, I began to worry. I went down to the barroom and a fellow named Jim Willie say he seen Feltie back of town at the Sweet Mellow wit' a yellow woman. I didn't like that, but I knowed the womens followed Feltie 'round, so I didn't think nothin' much about it. After that I had me a shot of scrap iron with a boy we call 'Fly,' and Fly say he heared this yellow gal tellin' Feltie how much she liked him and him tell her to go away and mind her business. Then Fly say she get real mad and tell Feltie she's gonna get even wit' him. I went on home feelin' pretty good and thinkin' Feltie was doin' all right.

"He come home late, and soon as I seen him I knowed he was sick 'cause his face was sort of red color. He say he ain't feelin' good, so I made him get in bed. Then I seen little yellow spots behind his ears. I took off his clothes and rubbed him all over wit' ammonia and water. That's the best thing to do when a man's drank too much scrap iron. But he kept gettin' worse and he feel like he's got somethin' in his throat that he can't spit up. He grab his neck and groan and say he's chokin' and for me to get a doctor. I called Dr. Williams and he come and look at Feltie and he say he's got pneumonia.

"That sure made me mad. I say, 'Doctor, you might know your business, but you is wrong.' I knowed by now what's the matter wit' Feltie. 'My husband ain't got no pneumonia,' I tell him. 'He's been hoodooed by a yellow woman!' Then I kind of lost control and I run out the house cryin' and carryin' on. I went down to the barroom and found a policeman and told him Feltie was hoodooed, but he jest laugh at me. Then I went back home and found Feltie as gray as that casket he's layin' in this minute. He rolled and rolled and jumped up and down, and I knowed the end was in sight. I lighted me some candles and I prayed, but it didn't do no good. I said, 'Feltie, you better pray 'cause you is gonna die.' That jest make him groan louder, so I knelt down by the bed and prayed for the two of us. Then Feltie started movin' his mouth and I saw he was prayin', too, although I couldn't hear no words. The children come runnin' in the room and I chased 'em. I was almost out my mind.

"Feltie was still livin' the next day, so I went back of town to see a hoodoo man named Father Joseph. He listened to what I said about Feltie, and then said my husband was full of snails and if I could get him to spit 'em up he might get well. I went back home and I sat by Feltie and I begged him to spit up them snails. He tried, but he couldn't get 'em out. I sure did pray then. Once I tried to get my hand down his throat to get them snails, but he jest hollered.

"It happened about twelve o'clock that night. I was sittin' by Feltie and rockin' and prayin' when he gave one cough and up come three big slimy snails and a little green frog. They hit the floor and they disappear. Me, I let out a scream and run clear to the back yard. When I come back Feltie was pantin' and groanin' and there was blood runnin' out his nose. Right after that he was dead.

"You know nobody wanted to touch his body? Even the undertakers was scared of him 'cause it spread all over town that before he died snails and a frog had come out of him. They was afraid all that bad hoodoo blood was still in him. I'm still scared, me. I been lookin' all over the house for stuff and I got a feelin' that yellow woman is after me, too.

"Last night that doctor come here talkin' about pneumonia.

I told him, 'Man, get out of my house and stay out. I knowed you ain't knowed what you talkin' about before, and I ain't listenin' to you now. I jest took you in 'cause you was a doctor.' He wouldn't believe I seen them things come out Feltie's mouth, but I seen 'em and I knows that Feltie Butler died a hoodoo death."

Negroes believe that tragedies such as that which overtook Feltie Butler are commonplace. For many years the curious belief that snakes, snails and frogs can be placed inside the human body to bring about ill effects has been widespread among them. It was said of both Marie Laveaus that they could thus afflict enemies, and today many illnesses and symptoms are believed by Voodoos to be caused by various living creatures inhabiting the human body.

Corinne Mothershed vowed that some evil Voodoo doctor had killed her mother. Corinne talked with her eyes closed when she told of what she had seen at the moment of the mother's passing. "I can't keep my eyes open when I talks about it," she said, " 'cause I keeps seein' it."

Her mother came home from church one Sunday night complaining of pains in her abdomen, according to Corinne. "My ma was a good Baptist," she said. "We never did have nothin' to do wit' hoodoo. She went to bed and slept, but the next mornin' she call me in her room and ask me to get a doctor. But before I could answer her she start havin' some kind of a fit. Her eyes rolled in her head and she screamed four times. Then, when that last scream come, little blue snakes began jumpin' out her mouth. I was so afraid I couldn't move. Them snakes hit the bed and the floor and they ran away as fast as they could move. When the last one had come up my ma was gone. Don't never let nobody say things like that don't happen. I seen it. About eight of them little snakes jumped right out of her mouth."

Corinne did not believe there was anything supernatural about it. "Somebody done give her snake eggs in her food," she said. "When they get big and want to get out her she die."

One of the most widespread of all such beliefs is that spiders sometimes come from the ears of people who have been Voodooed. Hattie Simpson had one sister who died this way.

"I been hearin' about that all my life," she said. "I seen spiders on the pillows of people what died—lots of times. They comes from the person's ears. When my sister started havin' her headaches I told her she was hoodooed and I wanted her to go see a hoodoo doctor, but she laughed at me. She didn't believe in that stuff and she ain't been around like me and ain't seen the things I've seen.

"The night my sister died, about two years ago, she woke up and started screamin'. When I got to her she was standin' up in her bed hollerin' like she was out of her mind. Then she just fell down on her face and when I reached her she was gone. Then I seen little gray spiders runnin' down her cheeks. I was scared sure then. I had been right all along. Some neighbor or somebody had *fixed* my poor sister. I never did nothin' about it 'cause I ain't sure who it was. And I never did know why they done it. My sister was no hoodoo. She was a good woman wit' a steady brain. I'll never forget how them spiders crawled out of her ears and then got away so fast. They was hoodoo spiders."

Hattie seemed to be a member of a very unfortunate family. She had another sister who was struck blind by Voodoo means.

"They sure *fixed* Adele," she said. "She was walkin' down the street and somethin' got in both her eyes. It hurt so bad she fell down and screamed. They took her to the hospital but she was blind. You know what they does. They kills a snake, lets him rot in the sun and then takes and throws the dust in a person's eyes. You see all kinds of little snakes grow in the person's eyes, and they can't see nothin'.

"I got Adele to a good hoodoo woman and she uncrossed her. She cooked some mustard greens wit' the juice from a dog's tail, put it in a bottle and shook it well. Then she made Adele lie down wit' her head on a pillow and she put about fifteen drops of this mixture in each of her eyes. In a half hour's time snakes was pourin' out her eyes. The hoodoo woman catched 'em in a bucket and burned 'em. Now Adele can see as good as anybody."

Consulted about the possibility of the dust of a dried snake causing blindness, a member of the Bureau of Scientific Research of the Louisiana State Conservation Commission stated that the venom of a snake is inclosed in glands within the snake's head. If the poisonous glands were dried along with the rest of the snake it was, according to his opinion, quite possible that the resulting dust might be capable of causing complete blindness.

Mrs. Desportes recalled what had befallen an intimate friend.

"This lady friend of mine made one of her neighbors mad," said Mrs. Desportes, "and a little while after that she became sick. I tell you, honey, she really suffered like hell. The truth was this bad woman wanted my lady friend's husband. My friend kept getting worse and she went to every doctor in town, but none of them could do anything for her. She died in the most terrible agony I ever saw in all my days. Her daughter had her opened up and they found a live crab in her stomach. All her insides were eaten away. Wasn't that terrible? I always will say that neighbor fed her that crab in some food when it was little and it grew inside her. Oh, it was awful!"

Many people believe that a Voodooed person may carry living things of the proportions of lizards, frogs and snakes under the skin in some part of their anatomy.

Joe Bezibon, colored, had a friend who developed a rising on one arm and sped in terror to a Voodoo doctor. The sorcerer told him there were lizards in his arm and he could be cured for five dollars. The victim consented, and the Voodoo doctor applied a poultice of lizard skin to the arm and gave him a brown candle to burn before he went to bed that night. But it did no good, according to Joe. "The man jest died and lost his money, too," he sighed.

"I remembers when I was a little girl," said Mamie Fonts, who lived in Pailet Lane, a Negro section of New Orleans near the Bayou St. John, "there was an old lady named Aunt Laura. She had snakes under the skin of her foot. You could see 'em crawlin'. Some hoodoo had boiled a lot of snakes and put the powder on Aunt Laura's foot when she was sleepin'. Sometimes they would crawl up her leg to her stomach and then she would vomit snails. It was awful. You know when she died—and this is the truth—you could hear a frog croakin' in her belly!"

Joe had seen much of such incidents.

"I had a sister who had a child hoodooed by a woman named Serena," Joe said. "That poor child used to bark like a dog, crow like a rooster, neigh like a horse and grunt like a pig. She was always runnin' around naked, and no matter what my sister did she wouldn't stop. Serena had *power* over her.

"Well, we got a man named Doctor Barkus to treat her. He always came in the house walkin' backward and cussin'. He was strong in the work. He'd walk up to this child, hit her over the head wit' his fis' and cuss her. After a while she got cured, but Serena always had *power* over her in a way. You know she made a hoodoo woman out of that child? She's real good, too. She went to Mobile to live and she's the best hoodoo woman they got up there. She can take a starched dress, stand it up on the floor and make it dance. She gets five dollars for a mojo. You know what a mojo is? It's the leg bone of a black cat that's been killed in a graveyard at midnight. I had me a good one once, but I ordered it from Chicago.

"And now I'm gonna tell you a secret," said Joe. "I want to warn you about this 'cause it's somethin' you ought to watch out for. When you drink anything out of a cup or glass always turn it upside down so everything gets drained out of it. Don't never leave a drop of water or coffee or nothin'. That is one way you get hoodooed now. There is still plenty of them people around, you know, but lots of other peoples forget that, and before they knows it they is in trouble. Some hoodoo done dropped some powder in their glass or cup, and it is too late to do anything about it. Me, I don't like ever to eat out at all. I guess everybody knows lots of colored people never eats in restaurants if they can help it. Plenty hoodoo workers are in those places, and you never can be sure the cook ain't being paid by one of your enemies to put *gris-gris* in your food. That's how peoples gets snakes and other things in their stomachs. Them hoodoos likes to work where your breath has been, too, and you don't even have to swallow anything. If they gets it into something you has ate out of, that is just as good. This is a secret, though, and most people don't never know it. Just remember you can't never tell who is a hoodoo and who ain't."

# 23
# Coffins on Your Doorstep

THE Voodoo curse is the worst of blights. Hex and all the other varieties of evil magic common throughout the United States do not compare with it. Hex and witchcraft and "ha'nts" can be controlled. They are usually of Anglo-Saxon origin, and, though they can be annoying, they are understood and familiar. Voodoo is of another race, dark and strange and complex even to those who practice it.

Orleanians have been finding *gris-gris* on their doorsteps for more than a century and a half. Long before the days of Marie Laveau crosses of death, tiny conffins, powders of peculiar coloring and composition have been found at dawn on stoops and galleries and in the front yards of the residents of the city. Sometimes there is a doll, jabbed with pins, sometimes a burning black candle, sometimes a wreath of crepe.

Fear of being "hoodooed" is the very core of Voodooism. Thousands of people fear a Voodoo curse as they do nothing else in the world. Negroes of the more ignorant strata live in daily dread of such a curse. Many whites of a similar element hold the same feeling toward it.

No law operates against the practice of Voodoo in Louisiana. There is an ordinance against fortune-telling in New Orleans, and in certain instances this can be invoked against practitioners. But though black magic and prophesying may sometimes be mingled, there is no real relationship between them. So, when a charge is brought against a Voodooienne—and this is seldom—it must be for malicious mischief or for disturbing the peace.

If the "fixer" is apprehended while placing some of the dreaded *gris-gris* on a neighbor's front porch and brought into court, the authorities cannot depend upon the victim to make any charge. He will practically always be too frightened, will sit silently, and will refuse even to admit knowledge of any such thing as Voodoo. He is afraid. He knows if the "fixer" is found guilty of whatever minor charge can be made, his punishment will be only the payment of a small fine or a few days in jail. Then the one who brought the charges will face an even more horrible curse.

Orleanians seek protection from evil *gris-gris* in many ways. The most common, of course, is the scrubbing of the front stoop with brick dust. Horseshoes nailed above doors are also popular. Roman Catholics tack "holy pictures" above their doors. But the most secure methods involve regular purchases from certain Voodooiennes of counter *gris-gris*, charms and amulets to be worn upon the person and kept within the home, involving the payment of small sums to these sinister merchants.

In most Negro neighborhoods there is a "hoodoo woman" or "conjure man," who enjoys to the utmost his superior position and the fear he inspires. Lala, though she says she does no "bad work," is an excellent example of this. Julia Jackson is another. Their neighbors fear them, but should *gris-gris* appear on any doorstep in the vicinity of either woman they will receive a visit from the victim, who will immediately purchase "protection" from them. And when a Voodooienne needs money all she has to do is to leave a small coffin or a black candle on a neighbor's stoop one night.

Sometimes the *gris-gris* is not left in plain view, but is carefully concealed; obviously in these cases the "fixer" is serious in his intention to bring bad luck to the victim. Believers in Voodoo search their premises periodically to make sure nothing is hidden beneath the steps or the flowerpots or in the small gardens in the front yards which most New Orleans residences have. However, most of the time it is left where it will be easily seen and will most quickly inspire fear.

Some of the believers do not have to find actual *gris-gris* to be terrorized. They are suspicious of any curious arrangement of the grass in the yard, of pebbles on the *banquette*, or of sticks lying in what they imagine is a peculiar arrangement. As often as not, anything of this sort will send them hurrying to the nearest Voodooienne or witch doctor, who will assure them that they have been *crossed*, and, for a certain fee, will agree to *uncross* them.

Despite all this, there is another and stranger attitude toward it all taken by some Negroes. Sometimes a *fixed* person will find masochistic pleasure in his condition. He will take to his bed, moaning and groaning that he has been "hoodooed." Soon he will be the center of attraction in his neighborhood. People will call, suggesting various cures and favorite practitioners. Finally some old woman will be summoned and she, after an elaborate procedure, will remove the curse. For weeks afterward the victim will still be the cynosure of all eyes whenever he appears. However, if his fear is too great, he may die. Then his family will enjoy a certain distinction for a long time to come. Gazelle received such notoriety from the strange death of Feltie Butler.

One summer morning in 1943 Dora Alberts, colored, found a conjure ball in her front yard. The ball lay in the grass, surrounded by matches shoved, heads downward, into the earth. Dora screamed and her husband, Thomas, came running out of the house. Neighbors assembled and held a conference, while Dora wept noisily. The matches represented tombstones—everyone agreed to that—and since a conjure ball was an omen of death, someone in the house was going to die. One brave woman, who claimed less faith in Voodoo than the others, picked up the ball, split the black wax open and displayed the human hair and the piece of flesh—undoubt-edly human flesh—concealed within it. This was the worst sort of conjure ball; it was a dreadful *gris-gris*. As the real-ization of what it meant became more intense all the women started weeping, and Dora fainted into Thomas's arms. Even the non-believer rushed home to wash her hands in a mixture of kerosene, whiskey and black pepper.

Dora remained in bed for days. At first she wept every time a visitor called. Then she stopped crying and lay in a deep silence, refusing to speak, at last also refusing to eat. At the end of two weeks everyone was positive that Dora Alberts was going to die.

Her husband called in doctors and each of them said the same thing. It was entirely a mental condition, a type of self-hypnosis. If Dora could be convinced that the conjure ball couldn't have done her any harm she would get well. But Thomas didn't even know what they were talking about, and, finally, though he had never taken much interest in Voodoo, he became convinced that the only way Dora could be saved was by the proper use of the same methods that had bewitched her. He began to question friends familiar with such things, and aid was not long in arriving. One morning a neighbor brought in a woman dressed in a long lavender robe and veil, and introduced her as "Mother Bertha."

Mother Bertha went to work at once. She drew a circle on the floor around Dora's bed with white chalk. Outside this circle she placed candles of various colors and lighted them. In between the candles she sprinkled certain powders. Now no more evil could reach Dora. Then she stripped Dora of her nightgown and bathed her with a mixture of jack honeysuckle, verbena essence and sweet oil. But that was not enough.

There had to be a cause, a reason why Dora had been cursed. Mother Bertha said that she would consult with Black Hawk and when this was found she could complete the cure.

Three days later she returned to Dora's bedside and told her. Dora related the rest of the story herself.

"She say it was a girl across the street, who wanted my husband," said Dora. "Right away I could talk and for the first time in nearly three weeks I opened my mouth and spoke words. 'Mother Bertha,' I said, 'I don't know whether it's your treatment or not, but I want to get out of this bed. You go on home. I can handle this hoodoo myself.'

"But I was too weak yet. Mother Bertha say I gotta eat and get my strength. Man, did I eat after that! I put down everything Thomas brought me and hollered for more. Mother Bertha come every day and talk to me. She told me Black Hawk had said it wasn't no fault of Thomas's that this gal liked him. He didn't know nothin' about it. So I didn't say a word to him. I just ate and got stronger and stronger.

"About a week after I had been *uncrossed* this gal come in to see me. You see, she had been comin' all the time—just like she was my friend. She come in this day and asked me how I felt. When she asked me that I yelled, 'I feel fine, you dirty husband stealer, you!' and I jumped her. I'm tellin' you I jumped out that bed like a tiger and I was on her. We broke up everything in the room. I was like I was crazy, 'cause there ain't no woman gonna take a man away from me!

"Next day I was up tendin' to my work and that gal was in bed across the street from the beatin' I give her. Then I got to thinkin'. I had to get rid of that wench for good. I knowed I could lick her again if I ever had to, but I didn't want to keep doin' that. That kind of a mess makes trouble, and sooner or later somebody lands in jail.

"I went to see Mother Bertha. I still owed her money anyway, 'cause she charged me plenty. She tell me to write that woman's name on a piece of paper and put it in a horse's mouth, and when the horse went away the woman would go away. Honey, I done just that. I got out early the next mornin' and catched the garbage man when he was passin' wit' his horse and wagon. When he stop to empty a can I went right up to his horse and shoved a piece of paper wit' that woman's name written on it in that horse's mouth. Then I run. You know inside of four days that wench packed up her stuff and moved? It sure did work. Mother Bertha called that St. George's work. You see, St. George always rode on a horse."

Letitia Brown told the story of Old Man Henry, a witch doctor who specialized in removing the curses placed upon houses by *gris-gris* concealed about the premises.

"Old Man Henry was one of the best for that sort of work," said Letitia. "He's still livin' and doin' his work, but he ain't got his snake no more so he ain't as good as he used to be. It was the snake that had the most *power*. The snake was named Henry, too. Ain't that funny?

"When people was hoodooed they went to see Old Man Henry and told him what had happened. He always called in the snake and made them tell it the story, too. That snake had plenty of sense, and he understood every word you said to him. Old Man Henry used to always say Henry wasn't a bitin' snake. Lots of peoples was scared of him, but he wouldn't bite. He was just like a human bein'. Well, after they told Old Man Henry and Henry their story, Old Man Henry would go to their house and put Henry under their front steps. Most of the time, you see, they wasn't sure they was bein' hoodooed—it was just that they felt kind of funny or somethin' like that. Henry would always smell around under the steps and all underneath the house, and if there was any *gris-gris* anywhere he would sure find it.

"After he found it he would go straight for the person who put it there, and Old Man Henry would follow him. When they found the *fixer* Old Man Henry would put a stronger curse on him than was on the other person, and everything would be all right.

"It was sure good work, and Old Man Henry did a big business. He never in his life has done any bad work either, except to get back at wicked hoodoo people. But now he's done lost Henry. One day a white lady was in her front yard and she seen Henry come down the *banquette* with Old Man Henry behind. She began hollerin' and yellin', and Old Man Henry told her Henry wouldn't hurt her and to stop yellin' 'cause Henry was scared of noise. But she keep on and she make so much noise Henry got sick. Old Man Henry nursed him and petted him all night long, but that poor snake never did stop tremblin' and shakin'. When the sun come up in the mornin' Henry was dead. Old Man Henry sure did grieve. He tried other snakes, but there wasn't none of 'em had the sense in his head Henry had."

Voodooists still mix their beliefs with some perverted form of Christianity. In New Orleans it is still often blended with Catholicism, probably because the city has always had a large Roman Catholic population. They adopt many Catholic saints as their own and invoke them to aid in Voodoo work. Besides this they have special saints of their own, these changing from time to time, old ones fading and new ones coming into popularity.

Black Hawk, stolen from the spiritualists, is, of course, the newest, but he had many predecessors. One of the earliest was St. Marron (or Maron). In slavery days he was the patron saint of runaway slaves, as well as of the Voodoos, and such slaves were known as "marons." Now he seems to have been completely forgotten. Another is Onzancaire, mentioned by Lala and known to many of the older Voodooiennes. However, he, too, seems to be on his way out.

Perhaps the most popular saint in the Voodoo world is St. Expédite, who, incidentally, is a peculiar example of the bridge between New Orleans Voodooism and Catholicism. Though his authenticity is more than doubtful, statues of St. Expédite are in at least two Catholic churches in the city, one of them Our Lady of Guadalupe, which is situated on North Rampart Street, almost adjacent to St. Louis Cemetery No. 1 and just around the corner from where the Laveaus lived. The church is a very old one and was originally the Catholic chapel from which all burial services were held. Both Maries must have known it well.

Priests, questioned about St. Expédite, remain noncommittal. Some will tell you they are certain he did exist. Others disagree entirely. There are no records. Some years ago Archbishop Shaw of New Orleans made a public and angry demand that these statues be removed from Catholic churches in New Orleans. But nothing was ever done, and the statues remain. Since then two Negro "Mothers" have opened St. Expédite temples.

But, whatever the truth is about his history, many Orleanians know that St. Expédite is the most dependable saint in Heaven when it comes to getting things done in a hurry. You have only to say, "St. Expédite, do this now." It will be done. Then you go to his statue at Our Lady of Guadalupe Church and pay off—sometimes by burning a candle before him and saying a prayer, but other times, if you're a genuine Voodoo, by leaving a slice of poundcake, a new penny or a sprig of green fern at his feet. Such articles are constantly being found before the image.

Octavia Williams believed that going to see St. Expédite was the best thing you could do if you found *gris-gris* on your doorsteps.

"He's the one can do the fast work," she said. "There is lots of ways you can keep from being hoodooed. You ought to always make a hole in a silver dime and paste a saint's picture on it and put it up on the transom of your front door when you move into a new house. But once you is *gris-grised* always call on St. Expédite for help.

"I done found salt on my steps one mornin', and right away I snapped my fingers and St. Expédite heard me. A woman across the street let out a scream and I found out later she had fallen off a ladder and broke her arm. She was the one what had tried to put a curse on me. You see how fast St. Expédite work?

"One time I was in my front yard and a man walk through the gate and just stand there lookin' at me. I said, 'What you want? Don't stare at me that way.' But he kept lookin' at me, and soon I felt I was gettin' under his spell. 'Go get me a drink of water,' he say. Now, I ain't never refused a drink of water to man or beast, so I went and got it. But when I come back he take the glass from my hand and don't say a word. He just hoodoo me some more wit' his eyes. I felt so funny I knowed I was gonna do anything he ask me. 'Go inside and get your money and give it to me,' he say. And I went on in and come back wit' all the money I had in the world—about seventy dollars. I just couldn't help myself. I gave it to him, and he asked me if that was all I had. I shook my head 'cause I couldn't hardly talk.

"Then somethin' happen. That man turned around and started to walk off, and you know the minute he had turned his head somethin' broke the spell. All of a sudden I got my sense. I yell, 'St. Expédite, help me now!' You won't believe this, but all of a sudden a two-by-four come flyin' through the air and that hunk of wood hit that thief on the head and knocked him cold. I grabbed my money out of his hand and start callin' my neighbors. They got the police, and that man is still in jail.

"Another time I done found a candle and a box of snuff

on my doorstep and I knowed what that meant. I went inside the house and opened the pillow I slept on and inside I found a hoodoo thing—a lot of feathers tied wit' string and a piece of red wax in the middle. I had to dump the insides of every pillow I owned in the river. I called on St. Expédite the whole time I was doin' this, and then I went and burned a candle to him at Our Lady of Guadalupe Church. Wit' all that nothin' ever done happen to me. That proves how good that saint is, don't it?"

# 24
# Easy Love and Easy Money

IN February, 1944, the Reverend Thomas Byron, who described himself as a Voodoo doctor, was charged by Federal officers in New Orleans with failure to register for military service in World War II. The reverend, known to Negroes as "Father Byron," claimed he could cure illness, heal cripples, bring love into lonely lives, and that his one aim in life was to help humanity and to give advice to "troubled people in this troubled world."

Father Byron, a very dark and serious-looking young man, wore the costume of a Catholic priest and operated a small establishment in South Rampart Street. On its plate glass window was printed the following:

| PUBLIC CONSULTANT | PUBLIC STENOGRAPHER |
|---|---|
| Personal Advice | Magazines and Novelties |

Father Byron did not depend upon his Voodoo talents alone to make a living. He also operated a small magazine stand, did typing for anyone in the locality, and sold such "novelties" as beauty preparations, patented medicines and other articles, which included candles, incense and the milder types of *gris-gris*.

Whether you seek money, health or love, the Voodoo doctors of New Orleans have always been ready to obtain it for you—for a price. There have been many famous ones of comparatively recent date, who have caused sensations in the

Negro world and pierced white consciousness sufficiently to win the attention of the newspapers, sometimes to attract the police.

Doctor Cat was one of the most prominent of recent decades. This wizard, whose real name was Joseph M. McKay, and who was by profession a dentist, seems to have been one of the most ambitious in the sect's history.

For Doctor Cat did not confine his operations to such clients as he could attract from the poorer elements of both races, but like the Laveaus and their contemporaries, he sought broader fields. An educated, light-colored Negro, Doctor Cat could not have been a serious believer in Voodooism. Doctor Cat wanted money. In 1914 he was operating a mail order business in the city, through which he sold advice, candles and *gris-gris* to all parts of the United States. He did very well financially. He had his wife's front teeth set with diamonds.

But Doctor Cat met the law at last. Federal authorities, armed with charges against him of having used the mails to defraud, appeared—and Doctor Cat left town in a hurry. He was arrested at Birmingham in July, 1914, after a two-months race with the agents.

Doctor Cat was a pioneer in mail order Voodoo. These businesses now protect themselves well by taking great pains to advertise their products as "novelties" and as being designed "for fun." Doctor Cat was much less sophisticated. He advertised himself as being able to "cure anything" and as "the man who can do anything you want done."

Troubles seldom come singly. When Doctor Cat was arrested in Birmingham he was not alone. There was a woman with him, a love he had taken there from New Orleans. Thus a Mann Act charge was also brought against him.

When he appeared in court the sorcerer insisted he was 127 years old, though he looked about 27. He went to a

Federal penitentiary for two years, his wife divorced him—
and nothing more is known of his fate.

Despite their fear of the law, many Voodoo workers have
been bold enough to advertise themselves. Marie Laveau II
distributed printed cards, offering her services, and they've
been doing it ever since. Back in 1913 Emile Laile, a particularly notorious practitioner, handed out cards that set a
new record for frankness. They read as follows:

EMILE LAILE P. H.

Meaning Professor of Hoodoo
All manner of Hants and Hoodoos removed
with neatness and dispatch.
No witch doctor is too strong for My power
References exchanged
Special attention to Emergency calls
Office, 2928 Orleans Street
My Office Hours Any Time
All Mail Orders Filled

Professor Laile found himself in trouble when he accepted
a fee from a white woman. She marked a fifty cent piece with
a pin, then notified the police. The professor went to jail for
obtaining money under false pretenses.

Sometimes witch doctors and Voodooiennes get into trouble
through greed, charging such exorbitant prices that their clients lose both their fear and their temper and notify the police.

One Negro, Willie Link, was arrested in 1925 for charging
twenty-five dollars for a small sachet of cheap powder, which
he claimed would render any man or woman helpless before
the amorous assault of the owner of said sachet. He allowed
his customers to buy the potent powder on time, five dollars
down, five dollars a month, until they had cleared their debt.
He was arrested as he took some letters from his mailbox.
One of the letters contained a five dollar money order.

In 1934 Wanda Carter, a Negress who admitted she was a Voodoo queen, was arrested in her home in uptown New Orleans. In her front room, on a center table, was a white bowl filled with cranberries. Wanda had been selling the berries for fifty cents each and had found many customers. They had special curative powers, she claimed, placed there by herself when she "blessed" them. Besides the cranberries, a varied assortment of *gris-gris* was found in her home.

In 1942 Bert Ellis was sentenced to a prison term after charging a man $150 to cure his son of epilepsy. The boy became permanently insane as a result of Ellis's Voodoo treatments. All the people involved in this case were white.

The most successful witch doctor of very recent years was Rockford Lewis. News of his activities first reached the newspapers in 1934.

Born in Thibodeaux, Louisiana, in 1905, Lewis came to New Orleans when he was fifteen years old. For a time he worked as yard boy and chauffeur for white residents of the city, including Mayor Semmes Walmsley, but later decided to go into the Voodoo business. In 1929 he opened a drugstore in lower Royal Street. Soon he was doing a large mail order business in Voodoo charms and powders and was becoming quite prosperous. Within a few years he had acquired a long, low, very shiny motor car, a liveried chauffeur, a flashy wardrobe and a huge diamond ring. He employed five secretaries and several other assistants.

Arraigned in Federal court in 1934, he denied any knowledge of Voodoo. The *Item*, after describing him as very black and with little education, quoted his statements as "I handles medals, sachet bags, lucky beans, lucky medals. Yes, sir, I believes in luck. I believes in helping people. But mostly I handles 'Save Your Life Rheumatic Oil.' I sells a lot of that." The last product had nothing at all to do with Voodoo, Lewis claimed, but was a valuable aid to suffering invented by himself in his own laboratory. One stenographer, called as a witness, testified that the mail orders they had shipped out of town had consisted almost entirely of the Rheumatic Oil.

C. E. Dunbar, a postoffice inspector, testified that he had sent money to Lewis from several places and had received various Voodoo charms in return. Once he had written Lewis that he wanted to obtain a position as president of a railroad and that the witch doctor had sent him some lucky amulets, perfumes and powders which were to be used in securing this position. Also presented in court was the following circular letter which Lewis had mailed to his clientele:

DEAR FRIEND:

I am writing you just to find out if you would like me to do anything for you? I can do any kind of work you want done. Let me help you out of trouble and give you luck and success in anything you undertake to do. I have helped people all over the world just by sending them the stuff to do all the work. Anyone can tell you my hands and tobies are good. Mail $5.00 and I will send the order. Anything you want done costs $5.00, state what you want done. Anybody in the world will tell you I am good.

NOTICE

If you tell your friends to write me I will make a discount for you.

Doctor Rockford Lewis received a sentence of two years in the Federal penitentiary at Atlanta.

In 1936 he returned to New Orleans and reopened his Royal Street business. His boldness in doing this startled even the Voodoo world. For a while, however, he remained content with a local trade, but in 1938 he again began selling his concoctions through the mail. A woman in Ohio wrote the Louisiana State Board of Health that she had been defrauded of some money through answering the Lewis advertisements, and he was immediately arrested again.

Doctor Lewis was not so wealthy now. Instead of the

luxurious limousine he owned a Ford which he drove himself and in many other ways he showed indications of less prosperity than he had possessed at the time of his first arrest. Yet he was able to employ a clever attorney and somehow he won this case and was set free with a warning. Years after this he told the story of the second arrest.

"I was in my laboratory fixin' my rheumatism medicine," he said. "I felt kind of funny, like it was gonna rain or something, and I knew bad luck was comin' my way. Still, when that knock came at my door I answered it myself, not thinkin' much. I opened the door and there was the policeman. And right behind him was other policemen. They come in and searched my house from start to finish. I was mad and I been through too much not to know my rights. I raised a fuss, and they told me about that woman in Ohio. Then they took me to jail. But I made bond and got out. I went and seen my lawyer right away and he say if I give him $1,500 to fix up a politician he know I would be all right. That was all right, but that was just the beginning. It grow and grow until I had given that lawyer and that politician $15,000 instead of $1,500. Of course it could have been worse. I got out of the trouble. The time before, I spent $18,000 and then went to jail for nearly two years."

But that escape seems to have cleaned out the last of Doctor Rockford Lewis's resources, and nothing has been heard from him in some time. Doctor Freddie Moses, a light Negro, popular on South Rampart Street, particularly in the night clubs and cafés, where he spends much money on drinks and the girls, expressed the opinion that Lewis should have done better.

"The trouble with Rockford Lewis was he didn't use his brains," said Doctor Moses, a much better educated man. "Voodoo is the smartest racket in the world. Lewis was a clever man, but he got to thinking nobody could touch him. You can't monkey with the mails because then you get mixed up with the Federal Government—and everybody knows you can't beat Uncle Sam. You have to be careful. If you advertise, everything has to be worded very carefully. People who use Voodoo treatments all over the country know what you're talking about without you having to talk too plainly."

The doctor fingered his neat mustache and one of his several diamond rings flashed. "You have to be careful about other things, too. One of them is women. I've fooled with a lot of women, but that's on the side. You can't mix them and your business. Women can't keep their mouths shut, for one thing. Yes, I know more of them practice it than men, but you have to watch them. Once they get angry with you, you're sunk. And they aren't reliable about paying their bills. You have to watch them. I never tell them a secret."

Doctor Moses admitted there would be little chance of making big money from Voodoo without some sort of mail order trade. "Voodoo is getting more popular every day in other parts of the country," he said. "If you stick to the New Orleans trade there is so much competition that you can't make a lot of money. There are a couple of real smart workers here. Take Professor Graham. That's a man who knows the Voodoo business and who knows how to keep out of trouble at the same time." He displayed a card advertising the services of Professor Graham. "Is there anything there about Voodoo?" he asked. "Not a thing. That's the kind of cards workers ought to use. If any police went after Professor Graham they certainly couldn't get anything from this card."

The card read:

#### WHAT DO YOU THINK ABOUT IT?
#### I KNOW ABOUT IT

You can get out of trouble and stay out. Your business place can be made good as anyone's and stay crowded. You can get your old job back again. Your love life can be happy.

## WHY BE DESPONDENT IN LIFE?

You can gain many Friends, get money and keep your apartments rented. So kindly consider all things are possible and there are wonderful blessings for everybody living. You may see—Prof. Graham—by appointment, only in morning hours.

"There is a man with sense," said Doctor Moses. "He doesn't say too little and he doesn't say too much. The people know what he's talking about."

# 25
# Medicated Magic

IT is difficult to win the confidence of certain South Rampart Street druggists, but it can be done. If you are white, the Negro merchants who sell *gris-gris* will almost never trust you; however, those white proprietors of the drugstores that specialize in Voodoo paraphernalia will talk quite frankly, once they are convinced you are not connected with the police.

"It's just like any other business," said one of these men, who owns a drugstore about a dozen blocks above Canal Street. "You sell 'em what they want; it's as simple as that. Not many of my customers come to buy aspirin or to have prescriptions filled. When I first opened up here I didn't know what this was all about. I thought I was going to have an ordinary drugstore, and when people came in here asking for Love Powders and Come Back Oil I didn't know what in the hell they were talking about. But I learned. When I was in school I didn't think I'd end up in the hoodoo racket, but here I am. There's money in it; I don't mind telling you that. It's a little dangerous, but not half as bad as booking the ponies or anything like bootlegging was."

On a counter near the entrance of this store is a stack of cards advertising all the more commonplace oils, waters and powders used by the faithful. Listed are Love Powder (white and pink), Drawing Powder, War Powder, Peace Powder. Controlling Powder, Anger Powder, Courting Powder, Mad Water, Angel's Delight Water, Black Devils Water, Hells Devil Oil, Love Oil, Mad Oil, Moving Powder, Easy Life Powder, 5th Century Grass, Lucky Jazz, Get-Together Drops,

Fast Luck Drops, Bad Luck Water, Lucky Lucky Water, Mexican Luck Water, Sacred Sand (all colors), Boss Fix Powder, Separation Water, Follow Me Drops and many others.

This large and florid-faced druggist also does a profitable business in candles, and he explains to some of his customers just what color candle they should use for each particular purpose.

"You're after some woman? Okay, take home this pink candle, burn it for nine days, an hour each time. You'll make her on the ninth night."

"You a gambler, boy? You want a blue candle. Burn it all night while you sleep and you'll dream of your lottery numbers."

"Got an enemy? Here's a brown candle; that's what you want for that kind of work. Put some sugar in a bowl, set the candle in it and burn it before you go to bed. Then take what's left and throw it in your enemy's yard." For some unexplainable reason Voodoos always have enemies.

This druggist sends out advertising circulars, some of them out of town, though he does no large-scale mail order business. These circulars state carefully that the articles offered are "novelties" and that no unusual claims are made regarding them, though "some people believe that they are good luck." Among others the following "novelties" are offered:

## FIVE FINGER GRASS

This plant has a leaf divided into Five Segments that many claim when hung up in the house or over a bedstead will bring restful sleep and ward off any Evil that five fingers would bring about. We make no claims to this effect and sell only as Genuine Five Finger Grass. Voodoos and certain Occults believe that each finger has a significance such as standing: 1 for LUCK, 2 for MONEY, 3 for WISDOM, 4 for POWER, 5 for LOVE.

ORDER BY NO. 2
PRICE ONLY ........................................ 25¢

## DRAGON BLOOD STICKS

Many of our customers like to carry a DRAGON BLOOD STICK as a CURIO. Some say it has brought much GOOD LUCK in Games, Business, Love Affairs and Money Matters. Many people prize this DRAGON BLOOD STICK and claim it is especially helpful when carried in the pocket or purse near their money and that it makes them REAL LUCKY. We make no claims to this effect and sell only as a GENUINE DRAGON BLOOD STICK.

ORDER BY NO. 3
PRICE ONLY ........................................ 25¢

## DIXIE LOVE PERFUME

Men are attracted by the delightful fragrance of Good Perfume. Down through the ages, the alluring fragrance of perfumes have played an important part in increasing the charm and beauty of womanhood. Many men like DIXIE LOVE PERFUME because its subtle fragrance seems to inspire Romance and Love. Many people say there is something Strange and Rare about this Perfume and that it seems to arouse the user with Passionate Fire, Love and the alluring Charms of the Spanish Señorita and Caballero. We make no representations to this effect and sell only as a very fine perfume. Enjoy this Exquisite Perfume. Buy a Bottle now.

ORDER BY NO. 9
PRICE ONLY ........................................ 25¢

## BRIMSTONE

Brimstone is burned by many people that believe in Black Magic, to keep away evil spirits, Voodoos and enemies, and to break spells that they believe have been cast on them. We make no claim but everybody is entitled to their own belief and no doubt get more or less satisfaction by using and doing such unusual things. Brimstone may be used in any way the owner wishes. It is fine to fumigate infected apartments, clothing, etc. You should not remain in the room while burning it.

ORDER BY NO. 12
PRICE, Per Box ........................................ 25¢

There are many others, all to be ordered by numbers only if you are an out of town purchaser. "We sell over a hundred hoodoo things," said the druggist. "Do they work? Hell, I don't know. They keep coming back for more."

Perhaps the best seller in this store is Wonder-of-the-World Root. And Wonder-of-the-World Root is truly a wonder. Used to locate buried treasure, it is sought most frequently by residents of rural sections who believe treasure to be concealed somewhere near their property. Louisiana is particularly rich in legends of treasure buried by explorers, Indians and pirates, and a certain percentage of the population is always devoting its spare time to unceasing efforts to locate these fabulous riches. Buyers of Wonder-of-the-World Root always buy a dozen or more of the roots at a time. The procedure in which they are used is very complicated, but the druggist had no objection to explaining it.

"The first thing you need," he said, "is Shem-Shem-Touras, the Tenth Seal of Mercury." He proudly exhibited a Shem-Shem-Touras, which he admitted he had made himself. It was a small piece of baby chamois marked with peculiar symbols in red ink. The treasure hunter digs a hole in the ground where he thinks treasure is located and buries the seal at least a foot below the surface of the ground. A few feet from this spot he plants Wonder-of-the-World Roots—one to the east, one to the west, one to the north and one to the south. This will "open the pores of the earth."

The treasure hunter now washes his hands in "Three Knaves Oils" and "Two Jacks Extract," then takes a small mirror and holds it over the place where the seal is buried. He is supposed to be able to see at least twenty feet beneath the earth. Next, he takes a willow stick, fastens a gold coin to the end of it and makes wandlike passes over the ground. This draws the treasure up to within four feet of the surface.

Has any treasure ever been found by using this method?

The druggist shrugged. That isn't his business. "You don't ask 'em questions," he said. "You got enough to worry about filling their orders. Voodoos are funny people anyway. I think I realized that most the night some vandals broke my show window. They ran off with everything I had on display—except the hoodoo stuff. They didn't touch that. They were scared of it."

The proprietor of another, and larger, Voodoo drugstore laughed at an insinuation that he might believe in it himself.

"But it surely is surprising how many people still do," he said. "The most unbelievable thing is how many white people come in here and ask for love powder and stuff to *fix* other people. I should say, roughly, that about one-third of my customers are white, the other two-thirds colored.

"Sometimes it does some good, though I know some of it is dangerous stuff. A lot, though, is just plain psychology. A Negro will come in here and say he's been hoodooed and, no matter what it is—just fear maybe—he is sick. I sell him some harmless powder to sprinkle around his house, and in a few days he's well again. I might sell him some aspirin, too, but he always thinks it was the Lucky Spirit Powder that did the job. I sell a lot of love perfumes and love powders, too, and if a gal's man likes the way she smells she gets him and they're both happy."

A slim Negro girl entered the store while he was talking, and he asked her what she wanted. The conversation that ensued was obviously typical of the day's business.

"I got trouble with my husband," she said. "It seems like I can't keep him home. I'd like some Stay Home Powder. Is that good, Mister?"

"Sure," the druggist said. "It'll do the job if you use it right. You know how to do that? You put it all over you when you go to bed with him. Rub it in good and he won't leave you. There're a lot of other things you've got to do besides that. You have to keep yourself nice and clean and bathe every day so you'll look pretty when he comes home from work. Do you always have a good dinner waiting for him?"

The girl admitted that sometimes they went out for hamburgers and beer.

"That won't do," the druggist said. "You got to cook a man real meals to keep him. Now how about some Controlling Oil?"

"Is that good?"

"Sure. You put some on your husband's body when he's asleep—just a little bit, not enough for him to notice it. You do like I say, and you'll have no more trouble." The druggist took two small packages from a shelf in the rear of the store and handed them to her. "That'll be fifty cents," he said. "Everything will be okay if you do like I told you." It was apparent that he was expert in giving out some practical advice with his *gris-gris*.

"Hell, it doesn't hurt to help these people," he said, when the girl had vanished down the sunny street. "They are just like kids."

A very black Negro was the next customer. He told of his fear of losing his job. He was a porter in a poolroom. "That white man I works for sure has got it in for me," he said. "I wants him *fixed* so he can't never lay me off."

"I have two kinds," the druggist said. "Which do you want? You know there's one that'll make your boss sick. You have to put that in his food. There's the other kind to make him itch."

The Negro grinned. "Ain't gonna do him no harm to scratch some," he said. "And he won't be able to do me nothin'."

"Okay," the druggist said. "I'll give it to you, but you

better put in a little hard work along with the powder. Don't you think you've been loafing on the job lately?"

"I guess I has," the Negro said. "Maybe I can do a little bit more work. The thing is I is always so tired."

When the porter had shuffled out the druggist said, "A combination of hoodoo and common sense does a right good job sometimes. It isn't going to hurt that man to get a dose of itching powder, but it won't hurt that boy to do some work either. I know him well. He hates to work and he stays home every Monday."

The proprietors of the Voodoo drugstores make almost all their own *gris-gris*. The powders and oils are usually very simple in content and are usually highly scented. Among simple people medicine must have a strong taste to be thought effective. Voodoo potions must smell. In general, good *gris-gris* must smell nicely, bad *gris-gris* should have a vile odor.

Love powder, for instance, is nothing but a talcum powder that has been colored pink or red and has been further scented with a few drops of a cheap but strong perfume. Perfectly harmless, it is a rather childish attempt to induce sexual attractiveness and is used for exactly the same reason that expensive white ladies use costly perfumes. Sometimes, however, its use is quite different. Some of its users throw it in the face of a person they desire. Others try to get it on the person's body or clothing. There are other love powders to be placed in food or drinks. Some of these are mild aphrodisiacs.

The oils and waters are usually also colored and perfumed, and with different colors and odors for various purposes. Fast Luck Water is ordinary water that can be purchased in many shades; red is for anyone seeking success in love affairs, yellow is for financial matters, blue is for protection and friends. Flying Devil Oil is olive oil, colored red, with cayenne pepper added; Black Cat Oil is machine oil; Love Oil is olive oil to which gardenia perfume has been added.

Anger Powder, War Powder and Moving Powder are composed of ordinary dirt, gunpowder and black pepper. Drawing Powder contains sugar; Controlling Powder contains salt.

All the Voodoo druggists sell candles of various sizes and colors. Prices range from five cents for very small ones to ten dollars for those large enough to be used in a church. The men who sell them differ somewhat on the significance of the colors, but most of them agree that white is for peace and to *uncross* people; red is for victory over enemies; pink is for love and for "drawing" people; green aids in the acquisition of money and will keep the landlord appeased; blue is for success and for protection from harm; yellow will "drive off" enemies; brown will "draw" money and help in gambling; lavender will bring harm to an individual one wants removed, and is useful to win out in a love affair; black, of course, is to do evil work and bring death to the person against whom it is burned. New Orleans Negroes, when having what they call "bad luck" or when feeling ill, will say, "Somebody is burning a candle against me." One small drugstore in South Rampart Street specializes in candles shaped like human beings. About a foot in height, they come in pink, red, blue, brown and black.

These merchants also sell pictures of saints. To certain Roman Catholic saints particular Voodoo power has been attributed: St. Michael is thought best able to aid in conquering enemies; St. Anthony de Padua is invoked for "luck"; St. Mary Magdalene is popular with women who are in love; St. Joseph (holding the Infant Jesus) is used to get a job. Many Voodoos believe a picture of the Virgin Mary in their homes will prevent illness, and that one of St. Peter (with the Key to Heaven) will bring great and speedy success in financial matters (without the Key to Heaven, St. Peter is still reliable in helping in the achievement of minor successes; the *power* of the picture is less, however). Pictures of the Sacred Heart of Jesus are believed to have the ability to cure organic diseases.

Of all the *gris-gris* in use today, though, the most popular is "Johnny the Conqueror." There are different kinds of Johnnys, and these have slightly different names, such as High John, Big John and several others, but every type is a twisted root with a pronglike formation at the end. One kind, with a long prong, is said to be a male Johnny; the other, with a shorter prong, is a female Johnny. For love and gambling the *power* of Johnny is considered supreme.

Abner Thomas will take an oath that Johnny the Conqueror is unsurpassed when used for sexual reasons.

"Good old Johnny!" he said enthusiastically. "If a woman ain't treatin' you right you just mix Johnny wit' cayenne pepper and sugar and put it under her bed. She is gonna love you like you is never been loved. If you think your wife is foolin' wit' some other man, you just put Johnny in her pillow. You ain't gonna have no more trouble. You can use 'em in lots of ways. I knowed a man whose daughter was foolin' wit' a married fellow, so he got a Big John and mixed it wit' goofer dust and red brick dust and put it under the married man's front steps. He say, 'Johnny, do your stuff!' and went away. It wasn't two days before that man come to him and broke down and say he was sorry he had gone wit' his daughter. Well, that fixed that, but the girl start grievin' and that worried her pa. He got him another Big John and soaked it in olive oil and placed it under the front steps of a fine young man in his block. A week later that young man was hangin' 'round wit' the gal and they got married. If you have any trouble wit' women use Johnny. He's a woman-fixer."

Abner also believed that Johnny was excellent for winning

at dice. "You keep it in your back pocket wit' your thumb on it," he said. "You tell it what you want to throw; you gonna throw it. You can depend on that."

Thousands of Negroes carry Johnny the Conqueror roots, not only in New Orleans, but all over the country, for enormous quantities of them are sold in Harlem, in Chicago, in Atlanta and Charleston, anywhere there is a large colored population.

"There is Big John and Little John," Abner said. "High John is the same as Big John; that is the strongest. There is male and female ones, too. Both of 'em has points, but the male Johnny has the longest and it's kind of rough. I always uses a male one."

The Johnny considered most effective is a Chicago product. Packed in a neat box, with a trade name known to all Voodoos, it sells for twenty-five cents. Many devotees will accept no other brand. "It ain't no good unless it's the right kind," they'll say. Advertising by this Chicago mail order house of Voodoo paraphernalia has convinced thousands that their Johnny is the "right kind."

Many users "sweeten" Johnny for success in love affairs. The root is soaked in sugar and water for twenty-four hours, then carried in the pocket when calling on the desired person. And Johnny is almost exclusively a man's *gris-gris*. Few women use it. "Johnny likes to help the men git the women," said Eddie Grecou.

Eddie had a very elaborate way of using the root.

"If you wants a woman," he said, "you buys a grapefruit, five cents of pink candles—them little ones they use on birthday cakes—some cayenne pepper, Epsom salts, some sugar and some salt. Cut the grapefruit in half, put it in a pie pan with the Epsom salts, sugar, salt and pepper all sprinkled on top the grapefruit. Write the woman's name on a piece of paper and stick this in the grapefruit. Now light your candles all around the pie pan, start walkin' round it in a circle, and, while you walkin', rub your Johnny the Conqueror and keep wishin' for that gal. You do this for nine days. On the ninth day she is gonna be your woman."

Eddie said that for gambling luck Johnny should be rubbed with olive oil and powdered sugar and then the end must be chewed. He had heard of people sprinkling love powder on Johnny, too. "But I don't believe you gotta do that," he said. "Johnny can take care of hisself. I know one thing that's true, though. If you can make a woman hold Johnny in her hand while you-all is layin' up in bed, then you is really got somethin'!"

Asked about lodestones, Eddie said they were "almost as good as Johnny for gamblin'."

And lodestones are probably second to Johnny in popularity. All the Voodoo merchants sell them, one drugstore advertising them as follows:

## LODESTONES

Used as Luck Charms by Many Who Believe
that They Cause Them To be Lucky
in Everything they Try to do.

This peculiar magnetic stone or ore has been used for ages as a LUCK CHARM and is now carried by many people who have implicit faith in its magic powers and who would not be without a pair of them.

They are sold in pairs, as many believers say that one piece drives evil away and the other draws luck. However, this is, of course, just according to your own belief, and our only guarantee is that we sell only

VERY HIGH GRADE, GENUINE MAGNETIC LODESTONES.

We buy our ore direct from one of the best mines. It is selected at the mine and again by us, giving you the best grade we can obtain.

We enclose it in neat chamois bags convenient to carry in the pocket, or strings can be attached so they can be worn on any part of the body.

OUR PRICE IS ONLY........... 50¢

This druggist also advertised the following accompanying ingredient:

MAGNETIC SAND FOR LODESTONES

This is pulverized Lodestone and while we make no claims, a good many people use it to feed their Lodestones.

PRICE ...................... 50¢

During the terrible influenza epidemic that followed World War I the Voodoo doctors and their clients and followers used the *power* to combat the spread of the disease. The *Times-Picayune* of October 20, 1918, wrote of the disappearance of vinegar from the kitchens of white residents and of a rite in which it was used by the Voodoos, who would recite "Sour, hour, vinegar—V! Keep the sickness off of me!" three times a day and would then bathe face, hands and sometimes clothing in the vinegar. This article also told of "making three crosses on the forehead before approaching a victim of the disease" and "the wearing of a white chicken feather on a cord around the neck." It also quoted the remarks of an old colored woman as "I'se got a horseshoe over my door, and a red string tied on de foot of my bed. I carries a dime in the toe of my stockin' and I rubs my chest with magnolia oil. I follers de signs and trusts in Jesus, and, praise God, I'se lived through three yellow fevers and one influenza an' I ain't daid yit."

But probably even more surprising than any of this was the custom of white Orleanians belonging to a stratum which would have scoffed at Voodoo of wearing a piece of lump camphor suspended from a string about their necks. Thousands of persons did this, and many still say it "kills the germs" and resume their camphor wearing in any winter that threatens to be one that brings many cases of grippe and bad colds. Undoubtedly the idea of wearing camphor for influenza started with some Voodoo doctor and reached the whites through their Negro servants.

If you wish to become a Voodoo witch doctor, here is the equipment essential to the opening of a successful business, with prices:

| | |
|---|---|
| Dragon's Blood | $ .50 |
| Love Powder | .25 |
| Sacred Sand | 1.00 |
| Black Cat Oil | 1.00 |
| Goofer Dust | .50 |
| Easy Life Powder | 2.50 |
| Boss-Fix Powder | .25 |
| Controlling Oil | .50 |
| Get Together Drops | 1.00 |
| Devil's Shoe Strings | .25 |

It is claimed by the Voodoo drugstores that all other powders and oils can be prepared from the same ingredients used in manufacturing the ones contained in this list.

Also necessary to the operation of a profitable Voodoo business are some effective costumes, a dingy room holding an altar on which are the essential candles, animal bones—if no human bones are available—and some pictures of saints, a somewhat mysterious facial expression and, preferably, an ability to tell fortunes, summon the spirits of the departed and make predictions.

"You gotta impress 'em," said Julia Jackson. "That is part of the business. They have more faith that way."

This is, of course, only the beginning. A Voodoo business

must grow like any other. When a clientele is established and certain miraculous "work" has been performed by successful usage of the above, the stock of *gris-gris* may be broadened considerably. One Voodoo merchant lists the following as being necessary to "the work":

| | |
|---|---|
| Love Powder, White & Pink | Moving Powder |
| Drawing Powder | Draw Across Powder |
| Cinnamon Powder | Flying Devil Powder |
| War Powder | Separation Powder |
| Anger Powder | Lucky Lucky Powder |
| Peace Powder | Good Luck Drops |
| Courting Powder | Mad Luck Drops |
| Delight Powder | Extra Good Luck Drops |
| Yellow Wash | Fast Luck Drops |
| Red Wash | Love Drops |
| Pink Wash | Drawing Drops |
| Black Wash | Luck Around Business |
| Lodestone | Robert Vinegar |
| Steel Dust | French Love Powder |
| Gamblers Luck | Get Away Powder |
| Van Van | Easy Life Powder |
| Dice Special | Goddess of Love |
| Incense (Vantines) | Lucky Jazz |
| War Water | Come to Me Powder |
| Mad Water | Goddess of Evil |
| Peace Water | Love and Success Powder |
| Mexican Luck | As You Please Powder |
| Angel's Delight | XXX 3 Cross Powder |
| Black Devils Powder | Lucky Floor Drops |
| Snake Root | Bend Over Oil |
| High John Root | Goofer Dust |
| Good Luck Powder | St. Joseph Powder |
| Hell's Devil Oil | Controlling Powder |

The list includes also candles, lucky bags and certain books.

And it is not necessary to purchase Voodoo equipment in New Orleans, for it is sold in all large American cities, though perhaps no merchant in other places has such a large and varied assortment as any one of the South Rampart Street establishments. However, much *gris-gris*—and but thinly disguised—is advertised in newspapers and magazines all over the United States, most often, of course, in those publications designed for and popular with the colored people of America.

In one edition of a Negro newspaper published in Chicago the following were offered: Magnetic Lodestones, Love Drops, High John the Conqueror Roots, Love Me! (a perfume, described as: "Heady! Exotic!"), Seal of Jupiter, Luck Hand Roots, Amulet of the Angel Phaleg, King Lodestones, Voodoo Night Perfume (the advertisement stated that "it D-R-A-W-S OTHERS!"), Lucky Seven Roots and the Talismanic Seal of Luck. Other advertisements invited the reader to send for their "Free Catalogs," that listed other charms, amulets, powders, oils, incense and candles.

Still other small boxes in this newspaper were headed "Know Thyself!" and "Do You Want Power and Love?" and "Do You Know How To Burn Candles?" One item read "New Orleans, the Psychic City!" and included an invitation to write a certain address in New Orleans for aid in acquiring "Power, Love and Luck."

Books on magic, astrology, numerology and outright Voodoo are also sold from South Rampart Street in New Orleans to the mail order houses of New York and Chicago. Some of these, such as *Ancient Astrology, Power Numbers, Dreams Revealed,* and *Ancient Mystical Prophesies* are only related to Voodoo in so far as they are popular with its followers, who combine all sorts of psuedo-science and superstitions with the more orthodox facets of the faith. But there are other books that are distinctly Voodoo. The South Rampart Street drugstores offer the *6th and 7th Book of Moses, The Art of Burning Candles, The Master Book of Candle Burning, Black Magic, an Explanation of Voodooism; Herb Magic, Mystic*

*Secrets of Mind and Power, The Egyptian Secrets of Albertus Magnus, or White and Black Art for Man and Beast* (this is the book known also as *Tit Albert* to Lala and other Voodoo queens of the present) and *The Life and Works of Marie Laveau.* All these books are paper-bound publications, and sell for from fifty cents to one dollar, with the exception of *The Life and Works of Marie Laveau,* which sells for three dollars and can be bought only in New Orleans.

*The Life and Works of Marie Laveau* is probably the most interesting of all the Voodoo books. On the cover authorship is credited to "One Of Her Descendants." An inside "Author's Dedication" is signed "Bivens, N. D. P." The blue paper cover is decorated with a pen-and-ink drawing of a woman with a pompadour that bears no resemblance to either of the Laveaus, and its forty-eight pages contain not a word regarding the history or activities of the famed Voodoo queens, but, instead, comprise some fifty descriptions of how to perform Voodoo magic. Each of these instructive paragraphs bears a title such as "The Lady Whose Lady Friends Spoke Meanly of Her," "The Lady Who Cannot Face Her Landlord" and "The Man Whose Wife Left Home." How to solve such problems is covered completely, though somewhat complexly. Despite all this, however, *The Life And Works of Marie Laveau* is a direct product and result of the activities of the greatest of the Voodoo queens and perhaps does actually contain some of their secrets.

# 26
# Murder!

VOODOO is not always harmless. It is true that much of it may be dismissed as ignorant superstition, spawned in a race of jungle people and carried with them to what we call civilization. However, that is not the whole story. There is bad *gris-gris*. Curses have been placed upon people, and the people have died. Voodooiennes and witch doctors have performed certain rites, and the persons against whom the curses were directed weakened and wasted away—or went mad. This was, and is, the real terror of Voodoo. It can kill.

A great deal has been written about the power of suggestion, and that may explain some of the mysterious deaths brought about by Voodoo and Obeah in the islands of the Caribbean, as well as in this country, but in those cases susceptible minds are required or no harm can result. The victim in each case must be a Voodoo or at least have some fear of it. If he is too worldly for this and laughs at it he is immune. All the tricks may be used, but the rotting fish with the victim's name inside, the tiny doll stuck with pins, the little boats floating on the surface of the Mississippi River and coffins buried with the prescribed ceremonies will be wasted. He will brush *gris-gris* from his doorsteps and kill *power* with ridicule and contempt. Despite this, however, deeply buried fears can often be uncovered in even the most disbelieving. If the Voodoo doctor persists it is surprising how much cynicism can be proved superficial. Somewhere beneath the veneer we all wear live superstitious ancestors—and if they can be reached the Voodoo doctor may win.

But there is something else, an easier way to kill that does not require any belief at all and is not nearly so much work. Poison! It was common gossip that the Laveaus used poison. When Antoine Cambre died in his cell on the eve of his execution he had eaten the Widow Paris's gumbo. Individuals cursed by Marie II sometimes died suddenly, and the people who knew the secrets of the Voodoos whispered of poison. On occasion this reached the ears of the police and an investigation of some sort was conducted, but never were either mother or daughter accused of murder by the authorities. The gossip was usually dismissed as the idle chatter of ignorant Negroes, according to some reports. There are other persons who will tell you that the police did not dare make an arrest, either because they were afraid of the Voodoos or because the political powers had been too well paid.

"I ain't afraid of no Voodoo," some Negroes will tell you. "I'm afraid of poison. If you got an enemy you gotta watch yourself. They use *gris-gris* on you all right, but the stuff they use is poison. If they can get some of that in what you eat it's too bad."

Voodoo can be a horrible reality. Many educated and intelligent persons know this. New Orleans families will sometimes see a favorite servant grow ill of some cause which no physician can ascertain, and she will take to her bed and die. Doctors at the Charity Hospital in the city are familiar with such cases.

It must be borne in mind that the happenings in the Negro world receive no publicity in white newspapers in the South unless they are extremely unusual or unless a white person is involved in some way. The Negro dying of a Voodoo curse in some tenement room in a back street may be the cause of great excitement among his neighbors, but this seldom pierces the walls about his own small world. The attending white doctor may wonder, but that is all. If he makes tests for poison

he will find none. This, the Voodoos claim when they are
boasting of their art, is because certain vegetable poisons that
defy chemical analysis are known to them. The doctor may
then decide that powerful psychological forces may have had
something to do with the death, but there is nothing he can
do. There is no publicity, and only the victim's immediate
circle know of the "hoodoo death."

It is almost exactly the same if the bewitched individual be
white, but of a very poor and obscure stratum of society. In
our social system publicity attends a person only in proportion
to how many other people know of his existence, his accom-
plishments (as measured by the standards of the system), his
real or imagined importance to the community and his wealth.
And if the white victim belong to a higher financial and edu-
cational level, his family will either have no belief in Voodoo
or will be ashamed to admit what they suspect. This also occurs
among Negroes of the educated class, who may be even
prouder than the whites of their freedom from all superstition.

Just as most crime is perpetrated by criminals upon other
criminals, most Voodoo killings are of other Voodoos. There
is always jealousy and feuding among them. Like all simple
people they frequently prefer to mete out their own justice,
and often there is a series of Voodoo deaths all stemming from
the same cause. A wronged woman or a jealous wife may turn
to Voodoo with results that bring death to her rival. Days
or weeks later the family of the dead woman will in some
mysterious fashion bring about the death of the one who
started the feud. Immediately after the demise of the first
victim the *fixer* will become conscious of the fact that she is
being *crossed*. Through power of suggestion, poison or some
other means she will become ill and she will die. No one will
know of the affair except the small circle in which both
women moved—and there has been no murder in so far as

the police are concerned. It is unlikely that they will ever hear of it.

The outright murders are the only Voodoo deaths that the public ever knows about. Now and then these receive newspaper publicity.

In 1938, in a parish not far from New Orleans, the Reverend Howard Randle cut his wife's throat because he believed she had put a spell upon him. His wife had been jealous of the colored preacher's female friends, especially members of his congregation upon whom he often called. In a moment of pique Lucinda visited a Voodoo doctor and purchased some powder to put in his coffee, the powder being supposed to have the power to render impotent anyone who consumed it. Randle drank the coffee, and almost immediately Lucinda lost her nerve and was overcome with remorse. She began to scream, "I've killed you! I've killed you!" Now the fear had come to her that the Voodoo powder might have even more drastic effects than the witch doctor had predicted. In a few moments she had convinced Randle that he was about to die. Now she fell to her knees and begged him to kill her.

The couple went walking out into the woods and sat down under some trees, Lucinda with her head in her husband's lap. She argued with him. He had been *fixed* and he was going to die. She didn't want to be separated from him.

"I figured I was gonna die anyway," Randle told the police later, "and I didn't want Lucinda left alone. She said she wanted to go first and that she'd be waiting for me by the river in that glorious land where we would live forever. I took out my knife and she closed her eyes. Then I cut her throat. It didn't hurt her at all. She just raised one leg, let it drop, and she was dead."

Lucinda may wait by the river a long time. Randle received a life term.

One morning early in the summer of 1939 a worker was walking through one of the older New Orleans graveyards when he saw a horrible sight. Wedged between two tombs was the nude body of a young Negress. The corpse lay on its back. A black hatpin was stuck upright in each of the breasts and in one of the hands was a curious *gris-gris* that consisted of a wasps' nest and some horsehair wrapped in red silk. She had been strangled.

She was at last identified as Margie Ellis, a resident of a downtown Negro section. "She been killed by some jealous woman around here," said Harry Ellis, her husband. "They was all the time accusin' her of messin' wit' their men, but it wasn't true. Margie was just a good-lookin' girl that the men liked, but she couldn't help that."

"Margie Ellis was a husband-stealer if I ever knowed one," said one of her female neighbors. "Her husband is tryin' to cover up. Sure some woman might have done it, but I bet she had cause."

"They got her with hoodoo," said others.

Everyone knew it was really Voodoo that had killed Margie. Someone had placed his hands on her throat and choked her, but what of the *gris-gris* in her hand and the black hatpins? At last an old woman named Rina Lee was arrested because she was going about the neighborhood boasting that she possessed secret knowledge about the crime. She admitted to the police that she had talked to Margie a few times and that Margie had thought she was being *crossed* by someone. Rina, well informed in Voodoo ways, was of the opinion that the person who had been responsible was a man in the neighborhood whom she knew only as "Bill." Rina said Margie had been going around with Bill a lot, then had suddenly decided to end the affair. After that Bill had disappeared from the section. Rina also said that Margie had loved her husband. "Margie was full of foolishness, but she wasn't what you'd call bad," was the way Rina put it.

After she broke with Bill, Margie began to find things. Crosses of salt appeared on the front steps of her home. She found a wax ball with hair in it under a fern in her front yard. That was when she had come to Rina. Rina had told her to bathe in Essence of Jack Honeysuckle and Peppermint, to burn certain candles and to make a Flying Novena at Our Lady of Guadalupe Church.

That was all Rina knew, so she was released and the police began to search for Bill. He was never found. "The spirits said he went to California," Rina remarked. "You know, what I can't understand, me, is how he ever got Margie to go to that graveyard. But she was always a kind of a crazy thing."

Now they say that Margie walks in that cemetery at night, a small naked ghost with long black pins jabbed in her breasts and the dread *gris-gris* held in one hand. Another legend has been born in New Orleans.

Rina, like all professional Voodooiennes, claimed to know many ways of killing people with black magic, though, of course, she vows she has never used her knowledge in this facet of the art. "There's big money in it," she said, "but I wouldn't kill nobody. You can still get five hundred dollars for hoodooin' a person to death. All you got to do is to put their name inside a fish wit' lots of black pepper and sew it up wit' black thread and bury it in their back yard. They won't last two weeks. Another way is to put their name inside a cow's heart wit' strong tobacco and bury it near the French Market. That's the same thing."

Though she didn't use it in Margie's case, Rina also claimed to be able to apprehend a murderer through Voodoo means. "If a corpse is buried wit' his hat on," she said, "the murderer will come back. Some peoples buries a murdered person wit' a cassava stick in one hand and a knife and fork in the other. That is a strong kind of work. I seen 'em put some of the killed person's blood in a jar and bury it in the north end of their back yard. The next mornin' the killer is gonna come to the door and confess his crime.

"I can catch a murderer any time I wants," she boasted. "One of the easiest and best ways is to bury the murdered person wit' a egg in his palm and put an eggshell on top his grave. In two days the murderer is gonna be down on his knees beggin' and prayin' for mercy. It's just knowin' what to do, that's all."

In 1932 a young Negro, Elijah Wheatley, pushed his girl, Lucille Williams, into a canal in lower New Orleans. A night watchman told police he had been attracted by the loud and angry voices of the quarreling couple and reached the scene in time to see Wheatley run away. The newspapers printed the story, so the police began a search for the Negro, who had vanished into the labyrinth of the colored underworld.

Meanwhile, Lucille Williams's body was recovered and the family prepared her for burial. A fresh egg was placed in each of her hands, a rope was tied around each of her wrists and she was laid face downward in the coffin. Then certain prayers were said during the two days and nights she was waked, and tall red candles were kept burning at each end of the casket. After the two days and nights she was buried and eggshells were sprinkled on her grave.

It worked. The first morning after the funeral the body of Elijah Wheatley was found floating in the same canal, and almost at the very same spot, where Lucille had drowned. The police, seeming a little embarrassed, offered the theory that the Negro had been overcome with remorse and had committed suicide. The Voodoos knew differently.

Voodoo probably drives its people to suicide more often than we know. The following happened back in 1928:

Someone wanted John Hall to die. This person bought from a Voodoo doctor a doll made of feathers. Each day this *fixer* unwound a small part of the thread that held the feather doll together. When the entire length of the string was unwound the doll would fall apart and John Hall would die.

Word reached John Hall that this was being done. He became ill. Friends shook their heads; he was a hoodooed man and had the "wastin' sickness." He became thin. His cheeks grew sunken, his clothes hung loosely on his body and his eyes were bright and feverish.

He prayed, but that did no good. Then he went to a Voodoo doctor and received instructions as to the only way he might save his life.

One Sunday afternoon he stepped out on the balcony of his home in St. Louis Street near North Rampart. In one hand he carried a tin can wrapped in a blue shirt. He said something under his breath and tossed shirt and can over the railing to the street, some twenty feet below.

A neighbor, Ethel Jackson, watched the little ceremony. She knew its meaning, and she knew what was to follow. But she didn't cry out or do anything to stop him because that would have transferred the curse to herself.

John Hall put one leg over the railing, then the other. Holding to the railing with his hands behind him, he stood balanced for a moment on the narrow outer ledge. He lifted his face toward the sky and he moved his lips in prayer. Then he jumped. Ethel watched his body fall to the *banquette* below. She still didn't scream or make any sound, but watched silently for a half minute. If he got up he would be free from the curse. At last the woman crossed the street and looked down at the crumpled form. Blood oozed from the skull. John Hall was dead. Then Ethel began to scream.

The most sensational Voodoo murder of recent years was among whites, not Negroes.

On April 1, 1940, at about 10:30 at night, an angry fist pounded heavily on the front door of the home of Salvador

Laurie in a quiet residential section of New Orleans. Laurie
and his wife were eating in their kitchen at the time. The
man rose, walked through the house, without bothering to
turn on any lights. His wife heard his footsteps as he approached the front door, heard the door open, then the re-
verberations of five shots fired in quick succession. As Mrs.
Laurie came running from the kitchen she heard an automobile engine start. Lights were flashing on all over the
neighborhood and people were pouring out of their houses.
On the steps Salvador Laurie lay dead.

The police were completely baffled during the investigation
that followed. There was no motive. Laurie had been a respectable citizen who lived a quiet and pleasant life, spending
most of his time with his family. Mrs. Laurie vowed he had
no enemies. He had never mingled with any criminal elements. There was no other woman in his life, so far as anyone
knew. Mrs. Laurie could think of only one thing that was
unusual. Lately Laurie had seemed very worried about something. He had even shown indications of a secret fear. He
had been very nervous for the past few weeks and had suffered from insomnia. When she had questioned him about it,
however, he had denied that there might be anything wrong.

One clue came from a man who worked with Laurie. He
said that the murdered man had told him of a rather strange
occurrence that had taken place some days before. Laurie had
said that one evening when he was driving home from work
someone had shot at him from another car. This had worried
Laurie a great deal, his friend said, and he had not had any
idea who would want to kill him or why. Laurie had never
mentioned this to his wife.

New Orleans detectives worked diligently. They carefully
checked Laurie's past, but nothing could be found that could
possibly relate to his being murdered. Apparently he had no
vices, worked steadily, did not drink or gamble. They even

went through their files to ascertain whether or not he bore any physical resemblance to some underworld character for whom he might have been mistaken. Nothing of this sort was found.

Almost completely on a hunch, and because he had recently bought a gun, the owner of a restaurant not far from the Laurie home was arrested. The revolver was examined by the experts and it was found to be the same type that had fired the bullets that had killed Laurie. People in the neighborhood told the detectives that the restaurateur had made threats against his wife. Recently the wife had disappeared and the man had been trying to find her, always taking the pistol with him. Then it was discovered that he frequently borrowed a 1932 model black Ford coupé with cream-colored wheels from his brother-in-law, Angelo Fratello, in which he drove about the city, trying to find his wife. Neighbors of the Lauries told of noticing a car of that description parked near the Laurie home the night of the murder.

It was all confusing. Had Laurie been mixed up with the restaurateur's wife? Careful checking convinced the police that this was not so. At last one of the waiters in the tavern was grilled. The man broke down and told of an argument between the owner of the place and Fratello the evening of the Laurie murder.

"Fratello was the one yelling about killing someone," the waiter said. "They really had it out. Once I passed the door of the kitchen and I saw 'em fighting over a pistol. The boss had it in his hand and Fratello was trying to take it away from him. Fratello left a few minutes after that, but the boss was nervous and excited for days afterward."

Faced with this story, the tavern owner at last told the truth. "Okay," he said. "Fratello killed Laurie. I was trying to take the gun away from him, not him from me. I should have told you before, but I didn't want to tell on him."

"Why?" was the question now. "Why did he do it?"

"I don't know," said the man. "He never would tell me." It was somehow obvious that he was telling the truth. "Angelo has been talking about killing Laurie for a long time," he said. "Maybe he's crazy."

Fratello was arrested and brought to police headquarters, but the detectives were almost as mystified as ever. It did sound like a case of mental derangement. Fratello and Laurie had scarcely known each other. No one had ever seen them together. All that could be discovered was that they had been friends as children.

But at last, after days of grilling, Fratello confessed. Slumped in a chair in the office of the Chief of Detectives, he mumbled dully: "Laurie had me hoodooed. He had put a curse on me." Becoming excited he began to shout, "I always wanted to kill him! He ruined my life! I was going to kill his whole family—his wife, his children, everybody!"

Slowly, painfully, sometimes bursting into childish tears, Fratello told the whole story.

"It happened a long time ago when we were kids," he said. "Laurie and a little girl we used to play with took me into a house down by the French Market. We went into an empty room and they did things that scared me to death and I tried to run away, but they caught me and brought me back. I began to cry, and then they said they'd put a curse on me.

"They dragged me out of that room and up some steps to a room where I could see a red light shining through the transom. They knocked on the door and it was opened by a big colored man who was as naked as the day he was born. He helped Laurie and the girl drag me inside. Then I saw the most awful things I've ever seen in my life.

"There were two other naked colored men in the room. They were sitting on the floor over in one corner beating on drums with their hands. In the middle of the floor a naked white woman was stretched out on her back on a sort of altar. Laurie and the girl pulled me down on the floor and we watched what went on.

"The man who had let us in took a rooster out of a cage and stood over the naked woman. The men in the corner beat the drums faster and faster and sang a crazy kind of song. It was awful! Then the man by the altar pulled the head off the rooster and let the blood spill all over the naked girl. She started screaming and he grabbed her in his arms and they fell together on the floor. The drums and the singing stopped.

"After a while the man got up and the girl lay there moaning and sobbing. She was covered with sweat and the rooster's blood, her eyes were closed and she seemed to be in a kind of spell. The man came over and picked me up and carried me to the altar. I fought him and screamed, but he was too strong for me. He took a bottle of some kind of oil and rubbed this oil all over. Laurie kept telling him to do a good job. After that we three kids left the house. All the way home I cried and trembled. Laurie said I was hoodooed now and I would be cursed for the rest of my life. That's why I killed him. I would do it again. Maybe now I'll have some peace."

The detectives stared. This was 1940, but before them sat a victim of a fear as old as Africa.

# 27
# The People
# Know the Signs

HENRY ALLEN, a Negro waiter at a New Orleans hotel, seemed glad of an opportunity to express his opinion about Voodoo. A serious, fairly well educated man, with intelligent eyes peering from behind gold-rimmed glasses, Henry's views were as representative as you are likely to find.

"My people all know about Voodoo," he said. "You must always remember that. Whether they believe in it or not, whether they're rich or poor, educated or ignorant, black or yellow, it is important to them. When they deny knowing about it they're lying because they're scared. I have heard that two-thirds of all Voodoos belong to my race and that the other third is white. I don't know if that is true or not, but I know that two-thirds of my people believe in Voodoo to some extent and that the other third treat it with respect. Of course those that believe in it have their differences, but when trouble comes they start looking for help from Doctor So-and-so or Mother Somebody-or-other and they get a little bottle of oil or some powders or something like that.

"Why that's all my people talk about! When somebody gets sick and starts to lose weight you'll hear them say, 'Have you seen Mary? She sure looks bad! I think somebody's got her *fixed*. You know she and Mildred ain't been getting along lately.

"Among my people any time two friends fall out they are suspicious of each other. They might treat each other nice and all when they meet, but they both wonder if the other person is *fixing* them. Soon as one gets a little sick—just a headache or anything like that—everybody who comes to see her tells her the other person must be *fixing* her. Hoodoo is one of the things my people live by. It's religion. When they need help they use it. When they want to get even with somebody they use it. They are always watching for it and guarding against it.

"I'm a Catholic, and I don't believe in any of it, but I had a brother who did. He was crazy about a woman and she wasn't doing right. He began to feel bad all the time and his friends all said this woman had him *fixed*. He went to Mother Kate and she told him he had snakes in his stomach. Well, she made him stay at her house all day and she gave him some medicine that was supposed to be hoodoo medicine but was really a strong purgative. She told him to stay in a room she showed him and to call her when he was ready to have a passage. He called her after a while and she brought him a bucket. He used that and then she showed him what he had passed. Of course she had dropped a handful of worms and snakes into that bucket, and he thought they had come from his own body.

"After that he believed in all that stuff. I remember one night we were all in church. I had gone to the Baptist church with my family that night—all my folks are Baptist; I changed to Catholic after I was grown. My mother got up to testify this night, and you know when you testify you got to sing. My mother never was a good songstress, so my brother started to sing to help her out. That woman he was living with touched him on the knee and told him to stop. He stopped, and that burned my sister up. As soon as church was over and we got outside the woman and my sister started fighting with shoe heels. You know lots of women of my race fight that way. They just pull off a shoe and go at each other, and those shoe heels are as bad as knives. My brother tried to grab his woman to protect her and I grabbed him, because I wanted my sister to give her a beating. When I grabbed his hand he screamed, 'Don't break my oil! Don't break my oil!' That stopped the fight because we were all so surprised. My brother had been holding a bottle of some kind of oil in one hand. He was going to rub this on his body to make his woman love him more.

"About a year after that my brother died. The doctor said he had ulcers of the stomach, but my sister always said that woman had him *fixed*. I don't know. I believe this: I believe if these hoodoo people can get to you they can put stuff in your drink or your food. That's why my people are always so careful where they eat. But I don't believe any hoodoo— or Voodoo, whatever you call it—can harm if the *fixer* lives across the river or ten miles away or anything like that. I think it's all poison. I've seen it kill people all my life. Of course I think lots of times a man is really sick of something else and people just say he's been hoodooed. But it ain't only the killings. I've seen people go crazy. I've seen 'em get down on the floor and bark like dogs. I've seen 'em waste away and get thinner and thinner, until they're skin and bones.

"Myself, I've never fooled with it. Sometimes I gamble a little, but I don't even carry a lodestone like most gamblers of my race do. The only thing I believe in is prayer. Lots of men, when they're playing dice, will say, 'Oh, Lord, help me make this pass!' but they're not really praying. When I say 'Oh, Lord, help me!' I'm praying!

"Like I said, Voodoo is part of my people. I think they need it. When white people mess with it, that's different. They're just ignorant or they're after something—like white gamblers will always carry lodestones, or most of them, anyway—but with my race it's something else; it's something to turn to when they're in trouble and it's something to use to get even with people who have done them harm. Of course maybe I just say this because I know more about my race. Maybe it's the same whether they're white or black.

"My grandpa used to always say something. I never did forget it. 'America,' he used to say, 'is just like a turkey. It's got white meat and it's got dark meat. They is different, but they is both important to the turkey.' I figure the turkey has more white meat than dark meat, but that don't make any difference. Both have nerves running through 'em. I guess Voodoo is a sort of nerve that runs mostly in the dark meat, but sometimes gets into the white meat, too.

"And it ain't only in New Orleans. I've been all over the country and I've seen signs of Voodoo almost everywhere, anywhere people of my race live. You can always find it. Of course lots of white people don't know anything about it, but we always know. Anywhere they go my people know the signs."

**THE END**

# Bibliography

"New Orleans, As It was," by Henry C. Castellanos.
"The Creoles of Louisiana," by George W. Cable.
"Strange True Stories of Louisiana," by George W. Cable.
"Creole Slave Songs," by George W. Cable.
"The History of Louisiana," by Antoine S. Le Page Du Pratz.
"Fabulous New Orleans," by Lyle Saxon.
"Old Louisiana," by Lyle Saxon.
"Louisiana State Guide," Work Projects Administration.
"New Orleans City Guide," Work Projects Administration.
Files of the following New Orleans newspapers:

> *Daily Delta.*
> *Weekly Delta.*
> *New Orleans Bee.*
> *Times-Picayune.*
> *New Orleans Times.*
> *New Orleans States.*
> *New Orleans Item.*

Files of the Writers Project of the Work Projects Administration at the Louisiana Library Commission.